What people are saying abc

"Is your life nothing like what you thought it would be? In *The Adventure: Discovering Your God-Given Passion, Place, and Purpose*, Adessa reveals that her life is very different than the one she imagined and dreamed of as a young girl. The reader joins Adessa on her journey from a life filled with dashed hopes and years of wondering what God's plan for her life was to a purposeful life of complete fulfillment.

Here is a beautiful truth: God has a plan and a purpose for your life. From the day you were born God had a design for your life that ONLY YOU CAN FULFILL!

Each chapter grabbed my attention with an engaging story and ended with thought-provoking questions that make this an excellent book study. With sound-scriptural truths and practical counsel, *The Adventure* will bring meaning, value and purpose to every believer's life and journey."

-Robin Immel, *Wife of the Superintendent of the PennDel Ministry Network and Director of the PennDel Women in Ministry*

"*The Adventure: Discovering Your God-Given Passion, Place, and Purpose*" is a must-read for anyone searching for God's direction in a confusing world. When life doesn't unfold like we expected, it's tempting to yield to disappointment or question God's plan.

Adessa writes with fresh vulnerability, weaving Scripture around poignant moments of personal testimony. She also provides opportunity for thought-provoking application, inviting us to know and trust Jesus in deeper ways. Adessa beautifully guides us to embrace authentic transformation."

-Angela Donadio, *Ordained Minister and Author of "Finding Joy When Life is Out of Focus: A Study of Philippians for Joy-Thirsty Women"*

"Adessa takes you on an important journey as you read this personal account of her life. You soon realize that God is working both in us and through us, even when life doesn't end up the way we had planned. The reading is easy, but the concept is often difficult for all of us to embrace; God is trustworthy with our lives. This book will help you walk down that path and you will be encouraged."

-Liz DeFrain, *PennDel Ministry Network Women's Director*

"We all have an inner desire to walk in the purpose that God created for our lives, however, many of us struggle to find this purpose. In *The Adventure: Discovering Your God-Given Passion, Place, and Purpose*, Adessa Holden shares her personal story of finding her purpose in God, supplying key advice and Biblical teaching on how to find your own purpose.

Adessa writes with brutal honesty of her struggle, allowing the reader to see she has lived what she preached. I highly recommend this book, not just to women, but to men as well who want to find God's passion, place, and purpose for their lives."

-Jamie Holden, *Founder/Director Mantour Ministries, President, 4One Ministries*

"Adessa's writing inspires us to move from tunnel vision to a flourishing mind set that is centered around God's unique plan and purpose for each of us. I commend this writing to you and to those within your circle of influence."

-Amy B. McClenithan, *Ordained Minister and Administrative Assistant at Central Assembly*

"Adessa's heart pours out on every page of this study. To say we need *passion, place, and a purpose* is one thing, but to live it is another.

Adessa draws us in through real life encounters that always brings us back to the Heart of the Father and what He is teaching us. Adessa not only inspires us to find our passion, place, and purpose but to go after it with all our heart...a must do study!!"

-Teri Rising, *Co-founder of One18 Movement*

"In *The Adventure: Discovering Your God-Given Passion, Place, and Purpose*, Adessa shares her struggles with disappointment and how God changed her thinking from, "How could you let this happen to me?" to, "How can I use this for you?" She shows the difference between knowing about Jesus and knowing Jesus. Adessa encourages the reader to embrace the truths God speaks over them and not listen to the world's lies. She's raw and vulnerable, sharing from her heart. Her experiences will challenge the reader and will help them become the woman God wants them to be."

-Suzanne Schaffer, *Author of "Simple Things", Pastor's Wife and Blogger*

"Adessa shares her struggles with finding God's passion, place and purpose. By sharing her personal walk, Adessa helps you to realize those disappointments and misunderstandings you need to deal with to help you grasp God's plan for your life. She helps you to pursue the abundant life God has for you. One of the subjects that touched me the most was living with a servant heart and being all that God wants me to be in the here and now. Thank You again, Adessa, for being transparent and challenging."

-Tina Roberge, *Pastor's Wife, Executive Director of Churches that Care*

"In this book, Adessa Holden helps readers understand that God's plans for their lives triumph over their greatest disappointments and challenges. She offers practical, Biblical insight on how we can align ourselves with God's heart to fulfill His purpose in our lives. She opens up and shares her own personal story of facing challenges and shows readers that God desires to first use us right where we are.

This is a great book that also includes thought-provoking study guide questions which help the reader think deeper and more personally. I would encourage anyone who reads this book to do so with an open heart."

-Crystal Knudson, *Children's Pastor, A Time to Heal Beyond Survival Regional Representative*

"Adessa has learned the secret for finding her purpose and fulfillment through some very real and hard personal experiences. She has an openness that is refreshing.

I believe God is looking for His daughters to stand up and move forward in their God-Given roles. The life lessons she shares in her new book, *The Adventure: Discovering Your God-Given Passion, Place, and Purpose*, will help us embrace the plans God has for us."

-Laverne Weber, *Laverne Weber Ministries, Author of "Victory's Journey for Women" and "Moving On for Men"*

The Adventure

Discovering Your God-Given Passion, Place, And Purpose

Adessa J. Holden

Published by 4One Ministries, Inc.

Design: James J. Holden

Subject Headings:

1. Healing —Religious aspects—Christianity. 2. Christian life. 3. Christian women—Religious life. I. Title.

ISBN 978-1-7338505-0-6 (paperback)

ISBN 978-1-7338505-1-3 (ebook)

Printed in the United States of America

DEDICATION

My Mom always said, *"Life is an adventure—you need to learn to love the journey."*

This is how she lived her life and she passed that attitude on to me.

For all of her support, her encouragement, her sacrifices, and her faith that God had a plan and a purpose even when NO ONE else did, I am dedicating this book to her.

Daily, Jamie and I reap the rewards of her spiritual investments. I will always be grateful to have taken this adventure with her and I can't wait for the day when we meet in Heaven and say, *"Look what God did! Who could have imagined?"*

I'd also like to dedicate this book to my brother Jamie—my co-adventurer. Ten books couldn't accurately tell the story of all that we've been through together. You will never know how truly grateful I am that you were and are here. I look forward to all of the adventures that God has for us in the future!

Also, I'd like to thank Courtney DiTrolio for her work as editor. Your perspective and attention to detail are invaluable. Thank you so much!

CONTENTS

Chapter 1

A NEW HOPE

When I was a little girl, my favorite question was always, "*What do you want to be when you grow up?*" The reason I loved this question is because I always had a very specific answer. I had always known exactly what I wanted to be—down to the very last detail—and I was more than happy to share.

You see, I was almost five years old when my Mom accepted Jesus as her personal Savior and began a relationship with Him. On a Sunday night a few months later, I begged her to let me go to church with her and our next door neighbor, rather than stay home with my Dad. As soon as she agreed, I ran to my room, pulled my Winnie the Pooh dress out of the hamper, and put on my black patent leather buckle shoes. Soon we were off to church.

I don't remember much about the service except that the sanctuary seemed so big and filled with so many people. (It was really just a small country church, but it looked big because I was so little.) I also remember there was a seeing-eye dog sitting in the aisle. This freaked me out because I was terrified of dogs, and here was one in church! (Thankfully, it left me alone.) Other than that, I don't remember much about the service, but something the pastor said must have made an impact on my young heart because that night after service, I went home, hid behind our sofa, and asked Jesus into my heart. Later that night I told my Mom what I did. She talked to me to make sure I understood what it meant, and then we prayed again. Even though I was very young, that night I had a genuine salvation experience that began my life of loving and serving Jesus.

A few years later, when I was only seven, I had another life-changing encounter with Jesus. It was another Sunday night, but this time a traveling Bible College ministry team was visiting. After they sang and performed some skits, their leader preached a message. At the end of his sermon, he gave an altar call for anyone who wanted to dedicate themselves to full-time ministry.

I remember practically running to the altar to answer the call, as the Holy Spirit moved on my heart. From that moment on, I knew beyond a shadow of a doubt that when I graduated from high school, I would go to Bible College to be trained to answer God's call into full-time ministry. I even took one of their brochures (which was ridiculous since it would be a decade until I would need it). Still, I held on to that piece of paper for years to remember that special night and my commitment.

After that night, answering the question, "*What do you want to be when you grow up?*" was pretty simple. I was going to be in ministry.

Of course, it would have been great if my answer had

stopped there. Only it never did. Over the years I added my own plans for exactly what my future would look like—down to the very last detail. It went something like this:

When I grow up I will be:

Married. I mean, obviously. How could I not be married?

Growing up in a small town culture where everyone married young and if you didn't marry there was something wrong with you, I naturally assumed that I would follow the normal pattern of going off to Bible College, getting married, and ministering with my husband.

Which brings up another reason that I was absolutely positive that I was going to be a wife. I grew up in a culture that had a less-than-Biblical theology about God's view of women. According to the belief system I was raised in, it was against God's will for a woman to minister unless she did so under the authority and supervision of her husband. Knowing that God had called me into ministry, I was sure that He would provide a husband so that I could answer His call. So I told people that I was going to be married and in ministry with my husband.

Yet, even that wasn't the end of my answer. As time went on and I grew older, I continued to add to my plan. One of my dreams that developed over time was that I wanted to be a writer. Yes, I was that artsy young girl who was always off by herself writing something. Whether it was lyrics to a song, the words of a poem, or recanting the stories of funny things that happened to my family and friends, I loved expressing myself through words. As I grew into my teen years, I began adding *"writer"* to the list of things I wanted to be someday.

Then came the day that I met THEM (by *"them"* I mean the most amazing pastoral team I have ever encountered in my life). I was around fourteen years old when I first entered their church. For me, it was love at first sight.

They were everything that I'd always thought a pastor and his wife should be. They truly loved Jesus and were wholeheartedly dedicated to serving Him and people. They were people of unquestionable character, very open and honest about their vulnerabilities and their strengths. They put their entire heart and soul into everything that they did, and every project, service, and presentation was done to the highest quality.

Professionally, they worked well together. He was the pastor, but she had a powerful ministry to women. Rather than being intimated by her, he allowed her to flourish and succeed in whatever God called her to do. I admired how they worked together and led their congregation, and if I'm being completely vulnerable, I'll admit that I was also attracted to their upper-middle-class lifestyle.

You see, there was another part of the fairy tale that I'd planned for my life that I haven't mentioned yet. Because even though I had genuinely and completely dedicated my life to following Jesus and serving in ministry, from a very young age I also planned to be very successful at it. In my vision for my life, I didn't plan on doing a lot of "*serving*" in ministry. Instead, I planned on being the next big thing. I imagined myself speaking to arenas full of women while I wore designer suits and lived in luxury hotels.

I planned on flying from place to place, ministering, and then going back to my big, beautiful house where my perfect husband and children would be waiting. When I looked at this couple, I began to believe it was possible.

Eventually, this became a problem. The more I observed this dynamic couple and sat under their ministry, the more I knew that this was what I wanted for my own life. I wanted to be them. Since their story already followed the outline I'd assumed God had written for my life, I determined that THEY were now my goal—who I wanted to be when I grew up. I absolutely had my heart set on it.

The only problem was that it was not God's will for me to have their life. His plan for me was completely different. Even though I headed off to Bible College with all of these big dreams and plans in my head, as I graduated from college, it became painfully clear that God's plans for my life were not the same as my own.

After four years in college, when graduation day came I was devastated that I was not married, engaged, or even dating anyone. I'd gone to Bible College and all I got was a lousy Bachelor's Degree in pastoral ministry. As a single woman, what was I going to do with that?

So on my graduation day, I was a jumbled ball of emotions. On a day that should have been a celebration of successful achievement, all I felt was overwhelming failure, heartbreak, and disappointment with God. When everyone stood to sing the old hymn *"Great is Thy Faithfulness,"* I had to fight back the tears that were trying to blast through as my heart was screaming, *"This is faithfulness? All I feel is let down, disappointed, and hopeless."*

As I packed my bags to return home from college, I felt like a complete failure. After years of dreaming about returning home as the successful heroic figure in every Hallmark channel movie, I was now returning to my small town not only unmarried, but also without a job. Because even though I had good grades in college, I'd worked hard, and done everything to pad my resume, God did not allow for one door of ministry to open. No matter how hard I tried, there was a God-ordained padlock blocking each door. The only option that I had was to return home with no idea of what I was going to do with my life.

I. was. DEVASTATED!

I remember telling someone that it felt like I was one pup from a basketful of puppies looking for a home. One by one, people came and chose a puppy, loved it, took it home, and made it their own. Only I was the last puppy left in the basket---the puppy that no one wanted. Not even God.

For the first time in my life, my future seemed unsure.

Until this point I'd always just assumed that my plans would be God's plans. Now I was faced with the harsh reality that this may not be true.

Now what?

Suddenly, I was asking questions like:

"If my life isn't going to follow the carefully laid out script that I created, what is going to happen?"

"What is my purpose?" "Where do I belong?"

"What does God want for my life and how do I get there?"

It was at this broken crossroads in my life that I began the quest to find my purpose—-the reason God had placed me on this planet.

Filled with fear, anger, frustration, brokenness, I began to ask, *"Does God even have a plan for my life?"*

I mean, I couldn't see it. Could I trust that God did?

I'm sure there are some who are reading this chapter and thinking, "*Uh, 'Des, don't you think you're being a little bit of a drama queen here? I mean, what's the big deal?*"

And yet I'm even more sure that there are many more who are reading it, and, although you may not be able to relate to the exact circumstance, you can certainly understand the pain.

You had a plan for your life—only life didn't turn out as planned.

Your perfect marriage ended in divorce.

Your dream job downsized, and you're not sure what you're going to do now.

Your plan for a big family was broken when you heard the word "*infertility.*"

You planned, and you dreamed, and imagined; you trusted God, and now NOTHING is turning out the way you planned.

Others may be reading this chapter and saying, "*I did get everything I wanted, but it isn't the way I imagined it would be. It didn't fill the void in my life, it came with challenges that I didn't expect, or it didn't give me the sense of purpose I thought it would.*"

Still others may be reading and saying, "*I had a dream, but I blew it. I walked away from God's plan, and now I have to live with the consequences of my sin and choices. How can God still have a plan and a purpose for my life?*"

Even though all of our circumstances are different, in our hearts we all feel the same.

Disappointed.

Confused.

Angry.

Heartbroken.

Lost.

Hopeless.

Purposeless.

Deep inside of our hearts, each one is asking the same thing, *"Okay God, what now?"*

To each broken heart God says: **"For I know the plans I have for you,' declares the Lord, 'plans to prosper you and not to harm you, plans to give you hope and a future." (New International Version, Jeremiah 29:11).**

Here is a very important fact that you need to know about this verse: It was written when God's people were in exile.

It wasn't written when they were living in their own land, living in peace and enjoying the benefits of being God's children. Instead, these words were written in a letter to Israelites who were suffering the consequences of a nation who had lost their purpose and turned away from God.

You see, the people of Judah were God's chosen people. They were the result of God's promise to Abraham in Genesis 13:14-17:

> **"The Lord said to Abram after Lot had parted from him, 'Look around from where you are, to the north and south, to the east and west. All the land that you see I will give to you and your**

> **offspring forever. I will make your offspring like the dust of the earth, so that if anyone could count the dust, then your offspring could be counted. Go, walk through the length and breadth of the land, for I am giving it to you." (NIV)**

The purpose of this nation was to be a people set apart for God. They were to live in relationship with Him, follow His Laws, and be a light to the people around them so that all the other nations would also want to follow God.

Only God's people did not follow God's plan. Instead, they abandoned their relationship with God and began serving the gods of the countries around them. Even though God sent prophets to call them back, time and again, and warn them of the consequences of their sins, the people continued breaking the covenant they made with God as His chosen people.

This left God with no other choice than to let them suffer the consequences of their actions, hoping that their heartache would bring them back to Him. So He allowed them to be taken into exile.

In exile, they lost everything....their land, their homes, the temple, and even their freedom.

From their perspective, it must've looked like God's purpose for their nation and their individual lives were over.

Yet, it was into this devastating, hopeless situation that God sent these words:

I still have a plan.

I still have a purpose.

You still have hope and you still have a future.

Today, I don't know what made you pick up this book. Perhaps you find yourself in the same place as the people of Judah saying, *"I made a mess of things, and I don't know if God can still redeem my life and make it into something beautiful."*

Maybe you're looking at your situation and saying, *"I don't know how this happened. I truly believed I was following God and trying to obey Him and yet nothing turned out the way I planned. Did I miss God's purpose? Does He have a plan? What is He doing with my life?"*

I still have a plan.

I still have a purpose.

You still have hope and you still have a future.

Maybe you've never had a relationship with God or thought that God had a plan for your life. You've looking for a deeper meaning in your life and trying to find your place in this world.

Whatever your situation, the promise of Jeremiah 29:11 stands firm.

God has a plan, a place, and a purpose for your life. You were put on this earth for a reason. God designed you specifically to fulfill that purpose.

Here is the best part: As long as you are breathing, you still have hope for the future.

As long as you are breathing, you still have hope for the future.

God still has a plan for your life.

You have a destiny that God wants you to fulfill.

Here's another amazing truth: God wants to share His design for your life with you.

It's not His will that you wander around trying to figure everything out on your own. Instead, the God of the Universe—-the God Who created you—-the God Who knows the past, present and future—-wants to walk alongside you every day of your life, leading you into the plan that He has for your life.

God is just waiting for you to decide to walk with Him and allow Him to lead you into His plan for your life.

Looking back, it was that decision that shaped my future and helped me find my purpose, my place and my passion in life. It was when I decided to stop chasing after my own desires and, instead, chose to follow God's plan for my life, that I started finding direction, peace, and the life that God designed for me to lead.

You can have the same testimony. It starts with the question, *"God, who do You want me to be now that I'm grown up?"*

Study Questions:

1. When you were younger, what did you dream about becoming when you grew up?
2. What made you choose to read a book about finding your passion, place, and purpose?
3. How do you personally feel or react when God changes your plans?
4. Read Jeremiah 29:11. How does knowing that this verse was written to people who were in exile affect your understanding of this popular Scripture?
5. The chapter says, *"God has a plan, a place, and a purpose for your life. You were put on this earth for a reason. God designed you specifically to fulfill that purpose."* What do these words mean to you?
6. Do you believe that God has a plan for your life?
7. How do you feel about the statement, *"As long as you are breathing, you still have hope for the future"*?
8. What is one truth you will take away from this chapter?

Chapter 2

PRECONCEIVED IDEAS

I used to call it my favorite house.

Every time I drove past it, I'd admire its shiny white bricks, the beautiful burgundy awnings and the landscaping that made the whole property pop from the road. For years I drove past it thinking it was my dream house. Imagining how great it would be to live in that house, I'd often comment, *"That's the house I want to live in someday."*

Then one day while I was driving by, I saw a *"For Sale"* sign on the lawn. Even though there was no way I could afford to purchase it, I just had to take the opportunity to check it out. I mean, if they took the time to hang those stunning burgundy awnings on the outside of the house, what must the inside look like?

Turns out, that the inside of the house was nothing like I'd imagined based on what I could see from the road. The layout was totally different. The landscape I'd *"oohed"* and *"ahhed"* over for years, ended up requiring a lot of maintenance. Even though the house looked pristine and perfect from the road, once you were inside, it had issues that needed to be repaired and addressed.

I have to admit, I was disappointed. When I actually got out of the car and allowed reality to meet imagination, I realized that this house was nothing like my preconceived ideas. Thankfully, I was only being curious and wasn't actually house-hunting. Could you imagine how much more disappointing it would have been if I was actually determined to buy that house? It would have been even worse if I'd been turning down other houses waiting for that one to go on sale! Had that been the case, I'd have been more than just a little disappointed—-I'd have been furious at myself for being so ridiculous!

And yet....

Over the past twenty years of my life I've observed that so many people make this same mistake when it comes to finding their purpose in life.

They get an idea of how things should be or they set their hearts on something they really want. Then they determine they must have it—no matter what. They get tunnel vision—- this is the way their life must proceed. There are no other options. If they can't have it this way, then they don't want it any way.

Personally, this was a HUGE issue for me. As I laid out in the last chapter, I had some pretty concrete ideas of the path my life was going to follow. I had it all planned out—-almost to the last detail. In my mind, there wasn't a lot of room for God to make adjustments. I mean, sure, maybe He could make tiny changes like the color of the big beautiful house I was going to live in or where that house would be located, but when it came to the big stuff, my plans were pretty much set in stone.

Only it turns out that my plans weren't God's plans. Instead, He had very different ideas. As a twenty-two year old woman, I was not really prepared to face His adjustments. When God changed my plans, I did not exactly respond with a chorus of *"I Surrender All."* Nope, I was ANGRY. I mean really, really angry.

I remember thinking:

"How could God let this happen? What could He possibly be thinking?

I had a plan for my life. I had goals. I probably even took the time to write them down, and I'm sure I sent Him a copy. Didn't He get the memo?"

This was not the way things were supposed to turn out!

Oh heck, let's get really vulnerable and admit that I was really thinking thoughts like:

"This is not fair. I don't deserve this. I played by all the rules---I kept up my end of the bargain. Sure I wasn't perfect, but I never did anything REALLY wrong."

I even compared myself to other people who hadn't kept God's rules as faithfully as I did (please understand those last few words were written with a roll of the eyes at my youthful, self-righteous attitude) and asked God, *"Why are their lives working out when they did this, this, and this? I didn't do any of those things, and I get nothing!"*

I was so angry and so hurt (these two emotions are usually pretty intertwined for me). Every ounce of emotion was being pointed directly at God saying, *"This is YOUR fault!"*

This went on for several weeks. Looking back, I feel so sorry for my family who had to live with me! I refused to unpack and accept God's plan. Instead, I tried everything I could to get out of the situation.

God didn't move (which just made me angrier).

Finally, my Mom strongly encouraged me to go to counseling with a pastor who didn't feel sorry for me, didn't pity me, and didn't even help me get out of my circumstances. Instead, he told me to start reading a book that dealt with the battleground of the mind. It was there that I started learning about the destructive power that preconceived ideas have in our lives. It didn't take long for me to recognize myself in each chapter.

The truth was that I had some very large preconceived ideas that were causing me to believe things about God that just weren't true. One of the biggest was the belief that a woman could only be in ministry if she was married and worked under the covering of her husband.

As a twenty-two year old single woman, this preconceived idea broke my heart and made me feel like God had rejected me. I felt that because God had not provided a husband, then He must be revoking His call to ministry. Since my entire life plan was based on the sincere belief that God had called me into ministry when I was seven years old and then renewed that calling over the summer when I was twenty years old, I was devastated.

I didn't understand what I'd done wrong. Why didn't God want me anymore?

How could He be so cruel?

Yet, the problem wasn't with God at all. The problem was that there was a massive preconceived idea in my mind blocking my ability to embrace God's will for my life. Even worse, this preconceived idea was trying to cause separation in my relationship with God and convince me that God didn't love me, and He didn't care about what happened in my life.

Looking back now I can see that, gone unaddressed, this preconceived idea would have derailed my life and kept me from the amazing plan that God had for me. Don't believe a preconceived idea could cause that big of a problem? Let's take a few minutes and look at the life of one of Jesus' disciples whose life was completed ruined by his unwillingness to give up his preconceived ideas.

Let's take a look at Judas.

When we first meet Judas, Jesus is inviting him to become one of His disciples—-to be among an elite group of twelve men who had the opportunity to spend every day with Jesus. What an opportunity! As a disciple, Judas heard teaching that no one else heard. He was privy to private conversations, probably some inside jokes. He was in the inner circle with the Messiah on the cusp of history. Jesus even trusted him enough to let him manage the group's financial affairs.

And yet for Judas, this wasn't enough.

As time went on we see that Judas didn't like the way Jesus was doing things. This whole *"discipleship"* thing wasn't going the way he planned. When it came to the mission of the Messiah, it was clear that Jesus and Judas were not on the same page.

Judas went into this *"following Jesus"* thing with some preconceived ideas. Yes, he believed that Jesus was the Messiah, but to him *"Messiah"* meant someone Who would deliver the Jews from Roman oppression, set up a kingdom, and rule the world. When that happened, Judas was totally prepared to be one of His top men.

However, things weren't turning out as Judas planned. Instead of creating a plan for world domination, Jesus was talking about dying and a spiritual kingdom. Day by day, it became clearer that Jesus had no intentions of doing what Judas thought He should do, and this made Judas angry.

This wasn't the way things were supposed to end! What was wrong with Jesus?

Why couldn't He see things from Judas' perspective?

As we continue to read the Gospels, we see that Judas' obsession with his preconceived ideas of the Messiah eventually caused him to make the worst decision of his life when he betrayed Jesus. Although this act ultimately became a part of God's plan, it destroyed Judas' life to the point that he could no longer live with himself after Jesus' death and committed suicide. In the end, he lost everything all because he couldn't let go of his own preconceived ideas.

"Well, I'd never make the same choice as Judas."

Yet here's the challenging truth: all of us have the potential to follow Judas' path because each one of us comes to Jesus with preconceived ideas. What determines whether the end of our story will resemble Judas' or take a different path is whether or not we are willing to let the Holy Spirit dismantle our preconceived ideas and replace them with God's plans for our lives. Are we willing to let the Holy Spirit show us truth from God's perspective even if it blows our preconceived ideas out of the water?

As a young woman, this was a decision I had to make. I had to allow the Holy Spirit to work on my heart and show me that many of the strong beliefs that I had regarding God's attitudes toward women were completely wrong.

Honestly, this wasn't always easy. Finding truth in this area meant facing that I grew up in a culture filled with abuse toward women. I had to see how false teaching from men who had problems with women had influenced my own thinking about God. It required many hours spending time with Jesus and studying the Bible so that I could see examples of how God really felt about women. It took facing truth. It took work, and an awful lot of tears as I allowed the Holy Spirit to dismantle this preconceived idea in my heart and mind and replace it with the truth that God could use a man or woman any way He wants in His kingdom.

Once this barrier was removed, I was free to start following God when He opened doors of ministry for me as a single woman. For me, the final hurdle of reconditioning my mind was when I applied and received my ordination as an Assemblies of God minister—-something I never even imagined would happened when I was in college because I was so caught up in the lie that it was against God's will for women to be ordained.

Of course, this wasn't the only preconceived idea that tried to keep me from following God's perfect will for my life. I had so many of them! Yet, as I allowed the Holy Spirit to point each one out to me and made the choice over and over again to abandon my preconceived ideas at the foot of the cross, God has been able to open doors that were beyond anything I could even imagine!

Now are things exactly the way I thought they would be? No.

Turns out that God's plan for my life was very different than what I planned. And yet, it's also pretty awesome.

Today, I serve in full-time ministry alongside of my brother. Although I never would have thought that God's plan would be for me to be part of a brother/sister team, we are actually a pretty dynamic duo, and I love working with him. As I said, because of wrong theology I was taught as a child, I never imagined that God would allow me to be an ordained minister with the Assemblies of God, and yet that was His perfect will.

Growing up, I never imagined that the ministry God had for me would begin on the internet (maybe because the internet hadn't even been invented yet). I never imagined how our books would reach men and women inside of prisons or the benefits of our podcast. Most of all, I never imagined, when God led my life on an unexplained and difficult detour, that my testimony would be used to reach so many hurting women.

When we are willing to lay aside our preconceived ideas and allow God to have the freedom to do whatever He wants with our lives, He really will do more than we can ever imagine or think.

You see, one of the biggest lessons I've learned is that when we are willing to lay aside our preconceived ideas and allow God to have the freedom to do whatever He wants with our lives, He really will do more than we can ever imagine or think.

But what would have happened had I made a different choice? What if I had refused to allow the Holy Spirit to dismantle the preconceived ideas in my mind?

What if I had taken the stance that if God didn't supply a husband, then I wasn't going to minister?

What if I refused to walk through the doors that He opened?

What if I taken the attitude that if I didn't have a writing contract with a big publishing company, then I wasn't going to write?

Although I don't know what exactly would have happened, I know for sure that I wouldn't be fulfilling God's purpose for my life nor would I be experiencing the joy and peace in my life that I have today.

God's vision is unlimited. While we can see options 1-10, God's options are infinite.

Here's the truth about preconceived ideas: They limit us.

They come from our limited experiences and our limited understanding.

However, God's vision is unlimited. While we can see options 1-10, God's options are infinite.

Because He sees beyond our present circumstances and into the future, He can look beyond what we think we need in the moment and say, *"No, this will be so much better for you five or ten years down the road."*

Because He knows us better than we know ourselves, He can look beyond what we think we need and give us what is really best for us.

Ephesians 3:20 says, **"God can do anything, you know—far more than you could ever imagine or guess or request**

in your wildest dreams! He does it not by pushing us around but by working within us, his Spirit deeply and gently within us." (The Message).

Those who are willing to take this risk and lay aside their preconceived ideas are in for the greatest adventure of their lives.

Unfortunately, those who are not—-those who cling to their preconceived ideas and demand their own way, believing they know better than God—will most likely end of in the same boat as Judas: far from God's best plan for their lives.

Personally, this is not the path that I want to take. Having learned from experience that God knows best, that He can be trusted, that everything God does is for our good and never to harm us, I continue to make the choice over and over again to lay aside any preconceived ideas in my life and take the risk of following God's will for my life.

What choice are you going to make?

Are there preconceived ideas that are keeping your from experiencing God's perfect will for your life?

Are they trying to distort your image of God making you believe that He is angry with you, that He doesn't love you or that He doesn't want what is best for your life?

Here's the most important question: Are you willing to lay these preconceived ideas at the foot of the cross and allow the Holy Spirit to speak truth into your life?

Ultimately, the decision is up to you. Do you want your way or God's way?

What is keeping you from wholeheartedly trusting God with your life? Are you willing to lay it down?

Looking back twenty years, I can honestly say that the choice to abandon my preconceived ideas is one of the best decisions I've ever made. It opened my life up to a world of possibilities that led to finding my passion, my place and my purpose in life. I hope you will make the same choice and exchange your preconceived ideas for all of God's possibilities.

Study Questions:

1. What is a preconceived idea?
2. How do preconceived ideas affect our view of ourselves, God, and the world around us?
3. How can preconceived ideas interfere with following God's will for our lives?
4. Can you identify any preconceived ideas that are keeping you from fulfilling your God-Given purpose in life?
5. How did preconceived ideas affect Judas' life?
6. How are we all like Judas?
7. How can we avoid making the same devastating choice that Judas made?
8. How do preconceived ideas limit us? More importantly, how are your preconceived ideas limiting you?

Chapter 3

SURRENDER

Several years ago I wrote a comedic sketch about what it would be like if Jesus and the disciples were riding in a mini-van heading toward their next speaking event. I imagined Jesus driving in the car while the disciples argued in the back.

"I'm the greatest."

"No, I'm the greatest....After all He picked me before He picked you....I have seniority."

"Yeah, well, I have more experience with real world affairs....what makes you think that a fisherman could help Him run the world?"

Then Nathaniel arrogantly says, *"Dudes, what are you arguing about. It'll be me. After all, when we met, He said, 'Now there's a real Israelite, not a false bone in his body'."*

From the back someone chimes in, *"I am so sick of that story, I think I'm going to gag."*

Finally, James and John pipe in, "Guys, stop arguing. It's going to be us....we're related to Him...we're familia." (I always imagine the sons of Zebedee having a Jersey mafia accent)

Sarcastically Matthew replies, *"Oh yeah, you two are going to be the greatest in the kingdom of God...the guys who had to have their mommy talk to Jesus for them."*

Can't you just hear all the disciples joining in to mock the mama's boys who had their mother try to have Jesus give them the position of sitting at Jesus' right and left hand in His kingdom?

I'm sorry if this seems too sacrilegious to you—-this is just how my brain works. It also reminds us that the disciples were just human beings with the same struggles we have with preconceived ideas about how our lives should be.

I believe it's important that we take a moment and realize that it wasn't just Judas who expected Jesus to set up an earthly kingdom and make him His top official. All of the disciples struggled with this preconceived idea. That's why they spent so much time arguing about which of them would be the greatest in the kingdom of God.

This includes Peter, the disciple we're going to talk about in this chapter. If anyone had reason to believe that he was headed for greatness when Jesus declared world dominance, it was Peter. We can only imagine what thoughts went through Peter's mind after this encounter with Jesus.

> **When Jesus came to the region of Caesarea Philippi, he asked his disciples, "Who do people say the Son of Man is?"**
>
> **They replied, "Some say John the Baptist; others say Elijah; and still others, Jeremiah or one of the prophets."**

> **"But what about you?" he asked. "Who do you say I am?"**
>
> **Simon Peter answered, "You are the Messiah, the Son of the living God."**
>
> **Jesus replied, "Blessed are you, Simon son of Jonah, for this was not revealed to you by flesh and blood, but by my Father in heaven.**
>
> **And I tell you that you are Peter, and on this rock I will build my church, and the gates of Hades will not overcome it.**
>
> **I will give you the keys of the kingdom of heaven; whatever you bind on earth will be bound in heaven, and whatever you loose on earth will be loosed in heaven."**
>
> **Then he ordered his disciples not to tell anyone that he was the Messiah. (New International Version, Matthew 16:13-20).**

Can't you just see Peter's chest puffing out after Jesus spoke these words?

What thoughts raced through his brain when Jesus said He was going to be the foundation of the church? Did he imagine power, fame, prestige, or the money he and his family would have? Seriously, stop and think about what it would be like to be Peter pondering the endless possibilities of the prophecy Jesus had just spoken over him.

Now take a moment and imagine the deep disappointment and disillusionment Peter must have felt when, instead of Jesus conquering the Roman government and setting up an earthly kingdom, Peter saw Roman soldiers carry Jesus away, beat Him, torture Him, and ultimately crucify Him.

What was Peter thinking as Jesus died?

How did he deal with the fact that everything he thought was going to happen was now beyond the scope of possibility? How overwhelmed must he have been as he saw not only his closest friend dying, but every preconceived idea of what it meant to be a follower of Jesus dying, too?

Alongside this disappointment, Peter was disappointed in himself.

Overwhelmed by the guilt of his own denial, Peter must have asked himself, *"How could I do it? Why did I deny Him? Why wasn't I stronger—I really thought I'd be strong enough to fight for Him. Why didn't He fight for Himself? How is this happening? What is God doing?"*

And then the ultimate question that we all ask ourselves in moments like these,

"What's going to happen now?"

You see, when we really get down to comparisons, Judas and Peter had a lot in common.

They both had preconceived notions about Jesus' mission as the Messiah.

Neither of them really understood God's perfect will for the world or for their lives. Ultimately, they were both disillusioned and disappointed in Jesus.

When push came to shove, they both made the biggest mistakes of their lives when they each, in their own way, betrayed Jesus.

And yet, their lives turned out so differently. While Judas

committed suicide, Peter went on to fulfill the prophecy Jesus gave over his life.

What made the difference?

I believe it was a matter of two men having very different hearts.

I believe that deep inside of Judas's heart, his motivation for following Jesus was really about what he could get out of it. When he realized Jesus wasn't going to conquer Rome, and the kingdom He spoke about was a spiritual kingdom, all of Judas' motivation was gone. Judas was about Judas—-his plans and his ideas of who the Messiah would be.

Peter, on the other hand, truly had a heart to follow Jesus. Even though he didn't completely understand God's plan when he agreed to follow Jesus, more than anything, Peter wanted God's will. As he spent more and more time with Jesus, he was convinced that Jesus was the Messiah sent from God. Even though he momentarily sinned by denying he knew Jesus, deep inside of his heart he loved Jesus and he wanted to follow Him. If that meant laying down his preconceived ideas and following God's plan for his life, then he was willing to do that....no matter what.

One thing I've learned throughout my life is that we're all a little like Judas and Peter. We all come to God with an idea of what *"following Jesus"* and *"finding God's will for our lives"* will look like. And, in time, most of us face disappointment when life doesn't turn out the way we planned. (I hate to be the one to tell you this, but most people's lives take different paths than what they planned or imagined. That's just life.)

What determines whether we are a Judas or a Peter is whether or not we are willing to lay aside our preconceived ideas and surrender our will to God's will. Are we willing to follow Jesus or are we just using God as a means to get what we want? It's this decision that tells us whether our hearts really love Jesus.

Over twenty years ago when I graduated from Bible college and all of the plans for my life fell apart, this is the decision I had to make.

The question now became, *"Was my life dedicated to following God's plan wherever it led or was I simply dedicated to fulfilling my own plan for my life?"*

Tough question.

I'll be honest, it's a question I've had to answer more than once over the last 20 years.

Being even more vulnerable, I'll admit that it's a question I didn't always answer correctly.

The truth is that it's hard for our deepest desires to die. As humans, we are wired to be innately selfish, to want what we want, and do everything that we can to achieve it.

When God comes into the equation and asks, *"Do you love Me enough to give Me your entire life, to let Me lead and guide you along the paths that I have for you, whatever they may be?"* there is a natural tug of war inside of our hearts.

Speaking from my own experience, I can say that whenever I have been confronted with this choice, there's always a part of me that wants to passionately follow God, throw caution to the wind and say, *"Wherever You go, I will go, too."* Of course, there's also the very human part of me that says, *"Will this get me what I want?"* (Just keeping it real here!)

The truth is that throughout my journey I've found that I am very much like Peter in Matthew 26:31-35.

It's the Last Supper, and Jesus has just told the disciples that on that very night, they will all fall away from Him.

As soon as Peter hears the words, he's shocked. Why, he would never! How could Jesus even think such a thing?!?

Didn't Jesus understand that Peter loved Him--- that he was *"all in"*---that He would do ANYTHING for Him? Wasn't Jesus aware of the sacrifices that Peter had already made?

Truly believing it to be true, Peter passionately replies, *"Even if I have to die with You, I will never disown You."*

The thing about Peter is that he truly meant it.

However, Jesus understood that there were some things in Peter's heart and mind that had to truly die before Peter would ever be able to stand behind the words that were coming from his mouth.

Peter's heart had to be broken. Peter needed to see that there were some parts of his heart that disloyal to Jesus.

Do I love Jesus enough to give my whole life to His service even if it means I don't get what I want?

Ultimately, in John 21, Peter needed to be confronted with the question, **"Peter, do you love ME?"**

Do I love Jesus enough to give my whole life to His service even if it means I don't get what I want?

What if Jesus' plan for my life doesn't even remotely resemble the dreams or aspirations I had for myself? Do I love Him enough to still follow?

You see, Peter couldn't keep His commitment to give up everything for Jesus until he first realized one thing: To follow Jesus, all of Peter's plans had to die.

John 21:17-19 says:

> **The third time he said to him, "Simon son of John, do you love me?"**
>
> **Peter was hurt because Jesus asked him the third time, "Do you love me?" He said, "Lord, you know all things; you know that I love you."**
>
> **Jesus said, "Feed my sheep. Very truly I tell you, when you were younger you dressed yourself and went where you wanted; but when you are old you will stretch out your hands, and someone else will dress you and lead you where you do not want to go."**
>
> **Jesus said this to indicate the kind of death by which Peter would glorify God. Then he said to him, "Follow me!" (NIV)**

"All to Jesus I surrender, all to Him I freely give".

The words are very popular; but living the sentiment is the greatest challenge you'll ever face in life.

It's easy to answer an altar call when you're seven and say, *"I'll follow You wherever, whenever, wherever, however"* but still keep a few caveats in your mind of what that really means. It's much harder to build a personal altar in your heart and say, *"Seriously, WHATEVER You want---even if it means that I don't get what I really want--- I love You enough to say WHATEVER."*

That's when things really begin to change.

The truth is that I don't have a story to go along with the day that I made a true WHATEVER commitment in my life. It didn't happen in response to an altar call or a dramatic sermon. I doubt that it was even an exact moment in time.

It was more of a process---a daily surrendering.

It didn't come during an anointed, Pentecostal moment, but rather, through many moments of pain, heartache and grief. It came choice by choice, decision by decision, hurtful comment by hurtful comment, through points of despair and hopelessness when it would have been easier to take the reins in my own life and say, *"I'm taking control now and doing what I need to do to get what I want."*

Each of us was created for the exclusive purpose of having a relationship with God and fulfilling the plan that He has for our lives.

During the times when that option was oh-so tempting, a quieter resolve was kept. Somewhere along the way, my answer to the cries in my own heart and the criticisms of others became, *"My life is not my own---I gave it away a long time ago. I will follow Jesus wherever He leads---even if I never get what I want."*

Somewhere along the journey I learned one of the keys to being happy and fulfilled in life: It isn't about me.

I was not created for the purpose of making myself happy by getting everything that I wanted. Each of us was created for the exclusive purpose of having a relationship with God and fulfilling the plan that He has for our lives.

Fulfilling that purpose is the ONLY way that you will

experience true joy, fulfillment, and satisfaction. It's the only road to finding your real value and worth. Even if all of the dreams that you have for your own life come true, if you don't have a personal relationship with Jesus and you aren't living out the plan He has for your life, you will never be happy.

We weren't meant to keep our lives, we were meant to find it by giving it away. (Matthew 16:25)

Does this mean you'll never get what you want?

Quite honestly, I don't know what God has planned for you. However, if what you really want is joy, peace, contentment, and satisfaction, what you really need is a change in perspective. You have to stop living for what you want and start seeking what God wants for you.

That's the key to living a life you will love.

It's the most crucial decision that you'll ever make.

Will you go along with God's plan for your life, whatever it may be, or will you do what you need to do to get what you want?

It's an age-old struggle---starting with Eve in the Garden of Eden.

She had everything; yet she chose to disobey God to fulfill her desire for the one thing she couldn't have. She didn't trust that everything God had given her, as well as everything He kept from her, was because He loved her and wanted what was best for her.

Daily, we all live with the results of her choice.

So often we think, *"Why did Eve make such a stupid decision?"* Yet, the same question could often be asked of us.

I don't know about you, but I don't want to follow in Eve's footsteps.

I want to trust God enough to lay my desires, designs, and questions aside and accept what He's given. I choose to believe that He is a loving Father Who gives His children *what* is best for them *when* it is best for them.

I want to follow Peter's footsteps and commit to following wherever Jesus leads, even if it means going where I don't want to go, simply out of love for my Savior.

Daily I want to make the choice to give my life away so that I can find a life that is more abundant that I could ever imagine.

Today I choose that all I really want, from this day forward, is Jesus.

Study Questions:

1. How were Judas and Peter alike?

2. What made the final chapters of their lives different?

3. Have you ever made a commitment to God, yet had your own preconceived ideas about what that commitment meant?

4. How do you respond when God's ways are different from your own? After reading this chapter, do you think you need to change your response in any way?

5. Read Matthew 16:25. How does this verse relate to the topic of surrendering our plans to God's plans for our lives?

6. What is the most difficult thing for you to surrender to God?

7. Do you love Jesus enough to surrender your whole life to His will, even if it means you don't get what you want?

8. List the areas of your life that you are choosing to surrender.

Chapter 4

GROWING PAINS

One of my greatest fears in starting off this book with chapters about abandoning your preconceived ideas and surrendering to God's will for your life is that it will appear that I'm promoting a daisies and gumdrops, name-it-and-claim-it, if-you-build-it-they-will-come approach to finding your passion, place, and purpose.

I'm not.

I'm well aware of the fact that a positive attitude and a spunky spirit won't heal hearts that are broken, comfort deep disappointments, or suddenly make us happy in unpleasant circumstances. (At least it never worked for me.)

Still, the reason I felt it was necessary to talk about these two topics first is because these two topics are the on-ramps to all of the other choices you and I need to make on our journey to finding our true passion, place and purpose. There will be days when we make the wrong decision to detour into depression, wanting our own way, feeling sorry for ourselves, or, God forbid, downright disobedience to God's will for our lives. But to get back on track, we'll once again have to pass through these two on-ramps and resurrender our lives to God's will.

Every person who has ever been serious about their commitment to surrender their lives completely to God understands this isn't always easy. Everyone who's ever been there and done that knows that surrender doesn't just magically happen.

It isn't natural; it isn't normal. You can't just pray a prayer and instantly never want your own way again. (Too bad, because that would be so much easier.)

> The naked truth about surrender is that it's a constant struggle to prioritize your love for God over your love for yourself.

Instead, finding joy through surrender comes at the price of daily decisions to lay down your desires, your plans, and your ideas and choosing to walk in obedience to God.

Sometimes the choice is filled with pain, and you have to choose to endure.

Other times the intensely human part of you rises up like a spoiled little child screaming, *"I WANT MY OWN WAY!"* and the spiritual man inside of you needs to rise up, take a stand, and say, *"No! Scream all you want but the answer is still 'No'."*

There will be moments when you'll get a bad case of the *"I deserves"* and even times when you'll be tempted to feel the *"that's not fairs."*

The naked truth about surrender is that it's a constant

struggle to prioritize your love for God over your love for yourself.

It's not always pretty; nor is it always easy. Even when you think you've got it licked, there will be days when you have to force yourself to once again choose: I will surrender my will to God's will and make good choices. You'll look in the mirror and say, *"I can't believe I'm still struggling with this issue,"* only to realize you've only got one option: Surrender again and tell your flesh to DIE ALREADY.

I know because I've been there…many, many times.

How much easier it would have been if I could have just said a prayer, surrendered my life to God, and instantly understood my identity and purpose in life. Only this isn't what happened. Instead, these discoveries came over a period of almost twenty years. It required daily decisions, over and over, to abandon the preconceived ideas of how I thought my life should be and once again submit to the plans that God had for my life in that moment.

You see, in between graduating from college and God opening the first doors for Jamie and I to start our own ministry, 4One Ministries, there was a period of fifteen years. During that time I lived at home with my parents. There were times when I had little jobs, and from time to time there were opportunities to do a little ministry here and there, but the majority of those days were spent walking through my very own, God-designed "Joseph experience." *(If you're not familiar with the story of Joseph, I encourage you to take some time and read about his journey in Genesis 37-48.)*

Even though this period in my life didn't make a lot of sense (to me or anyone looking in from the outside), here is one thing that I knew for sure: God had led me to this point in my life. Even though it looked terrible, I knew that God had led me to this place. Whether or not it made sense to me or anyone else, I knew that this was where God wanted me in this time in my life.

The other thing that I knew was that I did not want to be anywhere or experience anything except the center of God's will for my life.

Did knowing these two things make the hard times any easier?

Nope. Not at all. The truth was that even though I knew I was in God's will, it was still a really hard time.

At first, the most difficult thing to deal with was the humiliation. After all, I'd spent most of my life telling everyone who would listen about God's amazing plans for my life. Like Joseph in the Bible who told his brothers about his dreams that they would all bow down to him someday, I was a little obnoxious. As you can imagine, there were plenty of people who were happy to see me fall on my face and fail.

There were also well-meaning people who were genuinely concerned that my life had taken such a strange detour. Because I was feeling so insecure and embarrassed about my own situation, I took their questions and curiosity as insults.

Of course, I didn't need anyone to say anything positive or negative about my situation to make me feel bad. So much of my own self-worth was wrapped up in what I believed I would be someday. When I didn't reach my own aspirations, I was disappointed in myself. Because so much of my own self-esteem was wrapped up in keeping up appearances and people's approval, I was mortified and embarrassed that I hadn't lived up to everyone's expectations, including my own.

Yep, I had failed and everyone knew it....especially me. During those first few months and years when I was struggling so much with humiliation and embarrassment, my main goal was to make things look better—-to prove to others (and myself) that I wasn't as big of a failure as it seemed. This led to me running around like a mad woman trying to open any door and taking jobs that weren't God's will, only to have them end. I even briefly pursued writing music and spent way too much time and money trying to have the songs I'd written published. Meanwhile, God waited for the time when I would turn to Him and say, *"What did You want me to do?"*

Then once again, I'd abandon my ideas of what my life should look like and again surrendered to Him.

Eventually, I began to understand some of the reasons God orchestrated this season in my life. It was about a year after my college graduation that the Holy Spirit began revealing that there were things in my life and my past that needed to be addressed so that I could overcome and experience freedom. Over the next few years, we learned that my Dad had been lying to my Mom since the day they met and never stopped. All of these lies had a profound influence on our family, and all of us needed the Holy Spirit to do extensive work in our hearts to set us free. We literally spent years discovering truth, working through how that truth affected each of us, going through counseling, and learning new behavioral patterns.

Looking back, I can see that this was one of the greatest gifts that God ever gave me. Without this time, I would have lived my entire life believing lies, accepting abuse, and having an unhealthy view of God, myself, and relationships. However, once again I'd be lying if I said that I initially embraced this experience with arms wide open.

Sorry, that's not what happened. Instead, I didn't want to go through the pain. I wanted my own life and my own family, not to spend years overcoming the issues from generations gone by.

Once again, I had a choice to make. I could go along with what God was doing or I could run. I could give up on this process, take control of my life, and say, *"Enough. I gave God a chance, this is taking too long, I'm taking things into my own hands."*

Thankfully, I didn't do that, but I'd be lying if I said it wasn't a temptation. I'd also be lying if I didn't say that from time to time I tried to find an escape route only to be faced with the choice of obeying God and staying where I knew He wanted me or disobeying God and taking over the reins in my own life.

Looking back, I remember it wasn't always easy. And yet, I can say beyond a shadow of a doubt that I am so happy that I didn't run, that I kept choosing to follow God, and that I allowed Him to do what He wanted to do in my life.

Why?

Because it was through this process that I found my identity, my purpose, my place, and my passion in life. Even though I was worried back then about how things looked and whether or not God had a plan for what I would DO in the future, God knew that there were matters inside of my heart that needed to be addressed.

During this time I learned that it is not so much about what I do, but who I am.

My priorities were realigned, and I learned life lessons that I could not have learned through any other circumstances.

Now I know that this season was a gift. But it's a gift I never would have received if I'd followed my feelings and refused to give up my preconceived ideas and surrender to God's will over and over and over again.

So no, I won't tell you that finding your identity and purpose in life will be easy. I won't feed you a line that if you just say the right words, read the right book, and think positive thoughts, God will magically turn your situation around and give you the life of your dreams.

Instead, I will tell you that if you will choose to wholeheartedly follow God, even when it's hard and even when it hurts, if you choose to surrender and obey God's will for your life over and over and over again, then in His perfect time God will fulfill His dreams for your life. He will help you see yourself through His eyes and find the purpose He designed you to fulfill. If you will make this commitment, I promise that you will not regret it.

Make following Jesus your passion, and He will show you who you are and what you were created to do.

Today, I don't know what circumstances the Holy Spirit is asking you to follow Him through on your own journey to finding God's will for your life. I know that not many people will have the same story as mine, but perhaps He's asking you to work at a job that doesn't fit your dream position or to serve in a way that is different than you imagined. Maybe He has led you into a time of working on your heart and you're wondering, *"Why are we wasting time with this? I have a life to lead!"*

From the bottom of my heart, I encourage you to make the choice to follow God on whatever path He is leading you.

Don't demand your own way.

Don't run from Him in pursuit of what you think is better for your life.

Instead, choose to follow God wholeheartedly in whatever circumstances He places in your life.

Over and over again, be willing to give up your preconceived ideas and surrender your will to God's will.

Stay faithful in your time of devotions and keep reading God's Word. Be faithful in all that God has called you to do.

Even if it isn't always easy, I promise you that it will be worth it.

Make following Jesus your passion, and He will show you who you are and what you were created to do.

Study Questions:

1. How are *"abandoning preconceived ideas and surrendering to God's will for your life"* on-ramps to finding your passion, place, and purpose?

2. If you are unfamiliar with the story of Joseph, read his story in Genesis 37-48. How is Joseph's story an example of preconceived ideas and surrender?

3. Have you ever felt like God led you into your own *"Joseph experience?"*

4. Have you ever struggled with other people's opinions about the path God had for your life? What feelings has this caused? How have you dealt with them?

5. How do you feel about this line from the chapter: *"The naked truth about surrender is that it's a constant struggle to prioritize your love for God over your love for yourself"*? How does it challenge you?

6. What tempts you to abandon God's plan for your life and create your own path?

7. How do you resist the temptation to follow your own path? If you've fallen into this trap, what are some practical steps you can take to start resisting the temptation to take your life into your own hands?

Chapter 5

DESIGNED FOR RELATIONSHIP

"Do you love *me*?"

Have you ever asked God that question? I have.

During those first few weeks after my college graduation, I asked it a lot.

Yes, I knew that Jesus loved. I knew John 3:16 and had just spent years studying theology at Bible college. And yet, as I returned home from college deep inside of my heart I needed to know if God loved me.

Looking back, I think the question was really twofold. I was asking, *"Do You still love me even though I've completely failed?"* but also, *"If You love me, how could You let this happen?"*

From my place of heartache, disappointment, disillusionment, and brokenness, I needed an answer to this question more than anything.

So I turned to the only place I knew to find this answer. I fell back on a relationship that had been a lifetime in the making. I began investing more time in my personal relationship with Jesus.

You see, one of the greatest blessings in my life was that I grew up with a mom who taught my brother and I the difference between religion and relationship. Yes, she took us to church, but she raised us to believe that real Christianity was about having a personal relationship with Christ on a daily basis. She taught us that God wasn't just a part of our lives, but that, as Christians, our entire lives should revolve around Him. If we had a need, we prayed about it. When we were healed, we rejoiced. We talked about God all of the time, and she took every opportunity to teach us something about the Bible. Even when we were watching television, we talked about God's feelings on the show or what we could learn from it.

Throughout our lives, our mom encouraged us to develop our own personal relationship with Jesus. She taught us that our relationship with Jesus was as real as the relationships we had with our family. This relationship involved communication, emotions, and living our lives with Christ by our side.

Even when I was as young as six and seven years old, she taught me to have a designated time of prayer every day talking to Jesus about whatever was on my heart. Naturally, back then my prayers were very simple. I talked to God about my family, what was happening in school, and everything that was going on in my very limited elementary school life. Still, a relationship was being established, and even as a young child I was learning that Jesus was my best friend and I could talk to Him about anything.

As I grew older, my relationship with Jesus began to grow. The truth was that faithfully following Jesus during your teen years doesn't always make you very popular—even for a church kid. As I grew older, many of my friends began pursuing interests and ideas that I knew were against the Bible. Because of my love for Jesus and the relationship that we'd built, I didn't want to follow the same path. (Not that my parents would have let me!) This made my teen years very lonely, and many of my conversations with Jesus focused on my feelings during this time. We talked about how it felt to be a teenage girl, interactions with friends, drama with boys, and of course, what God wanted me to be when I grew up.

By the time I went off to college, I had more than just a casual relationship with Jesus. After years of consistently spending time with Him, pouring out my heart and finding direction and comfort in His Word, this relationship was strong. Even though I probably spent less time with Jesus in Bible College than at any other point in my life, I still found myself coming to Him over and over again looking for direction and finding time to tell Him every little thing that was on my heart.

One of the most special times that I remember during this period was over the summer between my sophomore and junior year. I had a summer job as a secretary at the PA Department of Commerce. Outside of the building where I worked, there was a park where I would go on most days and have lunch with Jesus.

During that hour we talked about everything. We discussed the boy who broke my heart, the fact that I felt so worn out from trying to impress people and be something that I wasn't, and my deep desire to be able to just be the woman God created me to be without trying so hard.

It was in this park that the Holy Spirit started the first of many discussions we would have about my family and the difference between my mom's personal relationship with Jesus and my dad's religion. That summer between noon and one o'clock, the Holy Spirit challenged me to make a choice: Who did I want to follow? It was also during one of those lunches that God reaffirmed my call to ministry and asked, *"Will you follow Me wherever I lead, even if it doesn't follow the path you laid out for your life?"* There, under the steps by the tree, I resurrendered my life. It was a beautiful moment.

Fast forward two years, and it was not such a beautiful moment. Instead, I was in a rather ugly place—-shocked at what God allowed in my life, disappointed, and feeling betrayed. Most of all, I was spitting angry. How could God let this happen?

I am not being dramatic when I say that returning home to my small town after college was my worst case scenario. I'd spent the last two years of college begging God not to let this happen and working very hard to make sure that it wouldn't, and yet now it was my reality.

After years of talking to God about this very issue and trusting that He would do what was best for me (which obviously couldn't be this), I felt completely betrayed by Him. Let's be honest, when I said He could do whatever He wanted with my life, what I really meant was anything He wanted except this!

I was at a crossroads. Completely filled with anger, all directed at God, I had a decision to make. I could walk away, give up and go back toward the casual Christianity I'd seen so many people choose. I could just go to church and make everything look good while I was really giving God the silent treatment and running my own life, or I could choose to hash this thing out with God.

Because I was not willing to give up my personal relationship with God, I chose the latter. Once again, I began setting aside significant amounts of time to have heart-to-heart talks with God. Let me tell you, they weren't always pretty.

But that's the beautiful thing about having a relationship with God—-you can say anything, and He can take it. You can tell Him exactly how you're feeling, what you're thinking, and unburden everything that's on your heart. I mean, let's be honest, it's not like He's surprised. He already knows everything about you—He knows what's in your heart. He has no problem with you sharing it with Him. In fact, He wants you to share with Him so that He can begin the process of removing the pain from your heart.

One of the biggest misconceptions that many people have is that when you pray you need to be very formal and only show your best self to God. They come to God speaking King James English or with their best Shakespeare impersonation, choosing their words very carefully as if they need to impress Him.

Others choose to become super Pentecostal and, instead of expressing what's really on their hearts, they shout and repeat super spiritual phrases over and over again trying to get God to hear them. Although neither of these types of prayers are necessarily wrong, they also aren't entirely necessary. While they both look very religious, they will rarely produce a deep, meaningful relationship.

Please don't misunderstand me—I believe in intercessory prayer and it has a very important place in God's kingdom. It's just not what we're talking about in this chapter.

Intercessory prayer is a form of ministry that you do, while building a personal relationship with God is a gift you give yourself.

After years of walking with Jesus, I've learned that you can't build a relationship by putting on religious airs, following a certain religious pattern, or trying to put on a big show (for God or others). No, a relationship can only be built when you let your guard down and just get real. When you allow God to see the good, the bad, the ugly, and the I-probably-shouldn't-have-said-that-but-oh-well-He-knows-what-I'm-thinking-anyway truth.

That's the kind of conversations God and I were having those first few months after I returned home from college. I was completely honest with Him, and He met me in the place of my pain.

Rather than being shocked or abandoning me, the Heavenly Father heard more than my words, He heard the cry of my heart. Day after day, we met, we talked, I cried, and He poured hope, healing, and a reassurance of His love into my heart.

Here's another amazing benefit of developing a personal relationship with God: He doesn't just listen; He speaks back to you. Because that's how conversations works—two people participate. Many days after I would pour out my heart, God would answer. Sometimes it would be though a Scripture that would seem to jump off the page, reassuring me of God's presence and that He was still in control or leading me in a certain direction. Other times, a still, quiet whisper would speak words into my mind. Sometimes it was just words, and other times He would literally place a song in my heart.

I remember one of the songs He gave me had these lyrics:

"I love you and you will always have a place in My house.

You can always walk with Me and eat at My table.

See I've prepared a place for you. I love you.

Just relinquish all your fear and your control.

I will never let you go. I love you."

Day by day as we continued to talk, the anger in my heart began to melt as I was once again reassured of God's love and His control of my situation. Not that this made me like my situation any more than I did before! Yet even though my circumstances didn't change, through times of dedicated, open, honest communication, my heart was taking the first steps toward healing, and I was regaining trust in the greatest relationship I've ever known—my relationship with Jesus.

Over the next few years life continued to be difficult as God's plan for my life and the life of my family took unexpected turns that I never imagined were possible. In time, I'd come to realize that the pain I felt when I returned home from college was really very small compared to the heartache I'd experience as we discovered my dad's lies, lived through his abusive temper tantrums, and watched my mom suffer from my dad's choices. In the years to come, we experienced medical crisis when my brother almost died of pneumonia and my mom developed severe environmental allergies. And yet through it all, I was never alone. The relationship that I'd built with God from the time I was a child, that was tested and reinforced in the days directly following coming home from college, was there supporting me.

As we faced each trial together, my heart changed. Instead of getting angry with God every time I was faced with a new challenge, I began to run to Him for help.

Rather than blaming Him, I began relying on Him. While my younger self said, *"How could You let this happen to me?"* as we walked through more and more difficulties, my response became *"I'll trust You to walk with me though this."*

Through every season, He proved Himself faithful. He was always there providing comfort, direction, and most of all proving that no matter what I was going through, I was loved.

Even through the most painful day in my life, when my mom fell into my arms and died, it was my relationship with God that carried me through. Through the strongest grief I've ever known, I knew that I was not alone. I knew that I could trust my Heavenly Father. I knew He was always there for me, and even though I again didn't have a plan for the future, He did. Because I'd learned to rely on His love, I knew that I could trust Him to be there with me through everything.

Spending time with Jesus isn't a "have to"—it's an "I get to."

That is the benefit of having a relationship with God. You're never alone. He's always there for you. As you walk through life together, He becomes your support system, the One you run to, the One you rely on, the One Who walks with you through each day, loving you through each step.

You know, sometimes I think we get so mixed up. So many people have such busy lives that they convince themselves that they don't have time to develop a personal relationship with God. They look at spending time with Jesus as a *"should"* or a *"have to"* rather than realizing it is the greatest opportunity of their lives. It isn't a *"have to"*—it's an *"I get to."*

While so many people see it as an imposition on their schedule, the truth is that building a relationship with God is the key to finding who you are and why you were put on this earth. Really, it is the very reason for which you and I were created.

Acts 17:24-28 says,

> **The God who made the world and everything in it is the Lord of heaven and earth and does not live in temples built by human hands.**
>
> **And he is not served by human hands, as if he needed anything. Rather, he himself gives everyone life and breath and everything else.**
>
> **From one man he made all the nations, that they should inhabit the whole earth; and he marked out their appointed times in history and the boundaries of their lands.**
>
> **God did this so that they would seek him and perhaps reach out for him and find him, though he is not far from any one of us.**
>
> **'For in him we live and move and have our being.'**
>
> **(New International Version).**

From the very creation of the world, God had one plan for mankind: a relationship. It was always His plan that our entire lives—-how we live and move and everything that we do—-would revolve around Him.

We see this laid out in Genesis 3 when God was coming to walk with Adam and Eve in the Garden of Eden. Even after their sin caused a separation between man and God, God was always making a way to restore our relationship with Him. In the Old Testament, we see Him reaching out to mankind as He set apart a nation for Himself and established a way for them to worship Him and be His people. In the New Testament, He sent Jesus to die on the cross, pay the price for all of our sins, and enable each of us to have a personal relationship with God.

The sad thing is that many people reject Christ's offer for salvation. An even sadder thing is that many who except Christ's offer of salvation, don't take full advantage of all that is available to them. They say a sinner's prayer, accept forgiveness of their sins and eternal life, but they don't take the time to experience the fullness of having a personal relationship with God.

In doing this, they are only hurting themselves. You see, God doesn't want you to walk through life alone. He doesn't want you to be on an endless journey, trying to find yourself, your purpose, your place on the planet, and something to be passionate about, on your own. Life was meant to have so much more meaning, but that meaning can only be found as we have a personal, intimate relationship with our Creator.

Life was meant to have so much more meaning, but that meaning can only be found as we have a personal, intimate relationship with our Creator.

The first step toward this relationship starts at the cross. If you have never accepted Jesus as your personal Savior, if you've never confessed your sin and accepted Jesus' forgiveness, then I encourage you to take a moment and do that right now.

Make the decision that I made so many years ago and say this prayer with me:

Dear Heavenly Father,

I come to You today and admit that I am a sinner and that my sin is keeping me from having an intimate, personal relationship with You. I thank You that You sent Your Son, Jesus, to die on the cross and take the punishment for my sin so that our relationship could be restored.

Father, today, I want to accept Jesus as my personal Savior. I want to begin having the personal relationship with You for which I was originally designed. I ask that You would not just forgive me of my sins, but walk with me through every moment of my life. Help me to understand Your love for me and find my purpose, my place and my passion in You.

I love You Father.

In Jesus' name. Amen.

Congratulations! You are now a part of the family of God. I am so excited for you! You are about to begin the greatest adventure of your life as the door is now open for you to have a personal relationship with God.

Please let me encourage you—-don't stop there! If you've just prayed that prayer, don't keep it to yourself—tell someone about it. Share the news with a friend who already has a personal relationship with Jesus. If you don't know anyone, contact us and we will help you connect with a local church who will be thrilled to hear about your decision and help you grown in your new relationship with Jesus.

Then, today—-right now—-take some time and talk to your Heavenly Father. Tell Him what's on your heart, how you are feeling, what you are thinking. Find a Bible (or a Bible app or go to biblegateway.com) and begin reading in the Gospel of John. Don't worry about reading a lot—just read a few verses and then think about what you've read. Do this every day and start developing your own personal relationship with Jesus.

Perhaps you're reading this chapter, and you've already accepted Jesus' offer of salvation, but you haven't yet taken the time to work on your own relationship with God. Maybe you've bought into the lie that you're just too busy or perhaps you're caught in the trap of religion and all of your conversations with God are very stiff and formal—- more of a business meeting than a relationship.

Can I encourage you today to make a different choice and begin developing your own personal relationship with God? It's never too late.

Just set aside some time to be alone with Him. Once you're there, be open, be honest, tell Him everything that's on your heart—-the good, the bad and the ugly. Talk to Him like a friend—like someone that you love, Who loves you back.

Then spend some time being still, listening for His voice to speak back to you. If you're not quite ready for that, start a daily Bible reading plan as a way for God to share His heart with you.

Most importantly, don't go one more day without taking the time to start your own intimate, personal relationship with Jesus. Realize that this was the reason that you were created—-to know Him and make Him known. The first step toward experiencing this and finding your purpose is developing your personal relationship with Him.

It's where you find all that you need and all that you were meant to be. It's the most important thing you will do with with your life. It's where you'll find your identity, your purpose, your passion, and the greatest love you have ever known—-in a personal relationship with Jesus.

Study Questions:

1. What is the difference between *"religion"* and *"relationship"*?
2. Why is open, honest communication important in developing a relationship with God?
3. Do you struggle with the idea that you can say anything to God and He can take it?
4. What steps can you take to overcome the preconceived idea that you need to be *"spiritual"* when you talk to God?
5. Does it surprise you to know that God wants to talk back to you? Have you ever experienced this in your own life?
6. How does building a relationship with God help you understand His love for you?
7. How does experiencing His love help you find your passion, place, and purpose in life?
8. What part of this chapter stood out most to you?
9. What practical steps can you begin taking to develop your own personal relationship with Jesus?

Chapter 6

DESIGNED TO BE WHOLE

One of my favorite movie scenes comes from the Tom Hanks film *"Castaway.*[1]*"* For those of you who've never seen the movie, Hanks plays Chuck Noland, a Fed Ex employee stranded on a deserted island after a plane crash that killed everyone else on board. After surviving at least 4 years on the island, Chuck manages to build a raft that takes him out to sea where he is rescued by a passing ship.

Then comes my favorite part of the movie: When he returns to civilization, Chuck is faced with a new reality starting with the fact that everyone had given him up for dead years ago. They had a funeral, and legally, he was dead.

Not only had his friends assumed he was dead, but his fiancé had moved on. She was now married with a young daughter (she sure didn't waste time!) In the over four years that he was gone, everything had changed.

Out of all of the dramatic footage in this movie, it was the last scene that left the biggest impression in my mind. After facing all of the changes and realizations that his old life was over, Chuck is faced with the question, *"What now?"*

After he delivers the one package that he didn't open on the island, he drives his truck to an intersection. Getting out, he stands in the middle of the intersection looking north, south, east and west. The movie ends with the unspoken question, *"Where do we go from here?"*

This is the same question that I found myself asking after I came home from college, re-surrendered my life to God's plan for my life and finally unpacked my bags. After I worked through my initial anger with God and choose to walk with Him through this journey rather than blame Him that life didn't turn out the way I wanted, I was faced with the question of *"Now what? Now where did I go from here?"*

Well, being a driven type-A personality, I immediately started doing everything I could to start knocking down a door---any door---to get me back on a life path that made sense. Knowing that this wasn't what I truly needed most at this time, God did not allow any doors to open.

Instead, He had a different path. He knew that the first priority was making some major repairs inside of me. After banging my head against a few too many brick walls, I finally caught on to the road that God wanted me to take and settled in for a time of repairs.

You see, what God knew (and I didn't realize) was that there were issues from my past and in my family's past that were keeping me from being the woman that He created me to be. These issues were influencing my identity, my sense of self-worth, and quite frankly, they were twisting my thinking about life, relationships, and even God Himself. Even though the next thing on my *"to-do"* list was find a way for my life to make sense again, the next thing on God's *"to-do"* list was dealing with my past so that I could find my identity as His daughter. The choice that He led me to next was, *"Are you willing to take a time-out and overcome your past?"*

I remember it like it was yesterday. We were driving home from church on a Sunday afternoon when the Holy Spirit starting revealing truth to me. The specific truth had to do with my relationship with my dad. For the first time in my life I was being forced to face the truth that it wasn't good, and it was having a profound impact on my life.

To be honest, I wasn't really shocked that my dad and I didn't get along.

Everyone knew that. My mom and brother always joked that we got along like a cat and a dog---always at odds.

The truth that the Holy Spirit was forcing me to see on this particular Sunday afternoon was that it wasn't my fault. Believe it or not, that was a pretty hard truth to face.

You see, even though it was obvious that my dad and I didn't agree on anything, I'd always blamed myself. (Mostly because my dad told me it was my fault.) I was rebellious. I was too driven. I wanted too much out of life. I was never satisfied. I was difficult.

My dad, on the other hand, wanted everyone to believe that he was basically perfect. He presented the image that he'd grown up in the perfect family where everyone got along and never fought. He understood life, relationships, and the world better than anyone else. He was the perfect Christian husband, father, and churchgoer. If anyone had problems—they weren't his---he was the victim. (Just a side hint I've learned over the years: whenever anyone has to be that *"perfect,"* suspect hidden problems lingering just beneath the surface. No one or nothing in life is perfect.)

Still, this was the pattern in our family. Whenever there were problems in the marriage (even a minor fight or disagreement), my dad said my mom had problems that she needed to overcome. When my brother and I had issues, we were the problem.

When my dad and I constantly butted heads because my type-A personality didn't fit into his definition of how a female should behave, I was the one who was being unsubmissive, rebellious, disrespectful, or unappreciative of how great he really was.

This pattern started when I was about 7 years old. I had just transferred from public school to Christian school, and I loved it! Right away, because of the different environment and the self-paced curriculum, I began showing a marked improvement academically. Not only were my grades very high, but I was moving through the work at an accelerated pace. Soon I was working at least two years ahead of my grade level and loving every minute of it.

My dad, of course, was not so thrilled. He was actually very threatened. When I did well, he felt insecure. His response was to assume I was cheating. He accused me of figuring out the system and moving through the work without learning. (This wasn't private; he also discussed it with my teachers.)

That pretty much set the tone of our relationship going forward.

The next ten years were basically a battle as I was being myself while my dad tried to squash my dreams, personality, and capabilities to fit into his definition of what a female should be. Of course, I was always wrong, and he was always right.

Instead of being proud and encouraging me to keep up the good work, his insecurities arose. The more areas where I excelled, the more he became hypercritical of everything I did. It was like he always had to point out that he was smarter by criticizing me.

When I became a teenager, he always told me I wanted too much out of life. He told me my standards were too high. Instead of supporting my dreams, he wanted to keep me in reality.

I couldn't do anything to please him. My personality was too strong. I talked too much and too loudly.

Eventually, my Dad's attitude toward me left me with a lot of confused ideas. Is this how God felt about women?

Did God really want women to squelch their personalities and capabilities to make men feel better?

Did all men feel the way my dad did?

By the time I graduated from college, these questions were tying me up in knots.

To a point, I had lost myself, trying to be the kind of woman I thought God and people wanted me to be. I was basically a chameleon, changing myself to fit in with whoever I was with at the time. The whole time the original me was all locked up in a box, while I was trying to be someone I wasn't. I wasn't happy, and God wasn't pleased.

It was time to face the truth.

I wish I could tell you that facing the truth was a once and done experience, but I can't. Instead, it was a rather long process of facing as much truth as I could handle, processing it, choosing to believe the truth instead of lies, forgiving, and learning new ways of thinking. It was kind of like an onion---there were many layers of pain and lies that had to be uncovered. With each layer, there was pain, truth, healing and ultimately freedom from the lies that were controlling me. Of course, as each layer was uncovered and healed, I also gained more and more freedom to stop believing lies, to lay aside the preconceived ideas that were poisoning me, and to start being myself.

Still, it took time. Over the next few years, the Holy Spirit revealed a lot of truth and uncovered a lot of secrets. We eventually learned that in his need to appear *"perfect,"* my dad had lied about almost everything in his life from the first day he met my mom. The truth was that he had a lot of issues in his own life that needed to be uncovered and addressed. Rather than dealing with them, he chose to use manipulation, lies, and abuse to control the people in his life.

That was his choice, but in the end, the people in his life (my mom, my brother, and myself) suffered the consequences. When the truth came out, each of us needed to make our own choice to overcome our past or let it control us and influence our future. Many times this choice required action.

Each of us had to choose to spend hours alone with God, praying through the issues of our hearts, and remembering things we didn't want to remember.

Then came the choice to forgive my dad whether he was repentant or not.

I had to choose to study the Bible to learn new behavioral patterns that I could apply to my life.

As a family and individually, we spent a lot of time in counseling and working with a minister trained in spiritual deliverance. There were so many knots that needed to be untied from all the years of lying, deceit, and abuse.

We did a lot of talking, and individually, we all did a lot of journaling.

The healing and overcoming wasn't magical by any means. It took a lot of work, and, honestly, choosing over and over again that we would allow God to take us through the entire process of overcoming our past and setting us free.

Although there were many years when I felt like Tom Hanks' character, stuck on a desert island just trying to survive, I have absolutely no regrets that I chose to allow God to take this time in my life and set me free from my past. Without a speck of doubt, it was one of the best choices I made in my life.

Why?

Because I couldn't become the woman God wanted me to be, (I couldn't even be myself), or do any of the things He wanted me to do until the lies and abuse that were scrambling my heart and mind were healed. Until I dealt with my past, I was broken. All I had to offer God or anyone else was my brokenness---a twisted, distorted version of the woman God had originally created.

When I chose to agree with God and allow Him to take me through the process of overcoming my past, God was able to heal my brokenness and replace it with wholeness and the opportunity to finally find my identity in Him. That's when things really started to change.

You see, as God healed my past, I was finally able to find something I didn't even know I was missing until that point: my identity.

Until I dealt with my past, I was broken. All I had to offer God or anyone else was my brokenness---a twisted, distorted version of the woman God had originally created.

When the truth came out that my dad had lots of unresolved issues from his own life that were affecting his ideas about women, I was finally able to stop twisting my personality into what he wanted it to be. When the Holy Spirit revealed that my dad's ideas about men and women, submission and relationships were wrong, I was able to take a deep breath and realize that I was not the problem. God created me exactly the way He wanted me to be to accomplish His plan for my life. I could stop trying to squash, kill, hide, or distort my personality to fit my dad's crazy ideas, and just be myself.

It was like breathing fresh air for the first time.

Once the truth came out, I was finally allowed to start loving myself---just the way I was, flaws and all. I began realizing that the only person I needed to care about pleasing was God. He liked me just the way I was---after all, He created me that way.

Sure, there were parts of me that He wanted to refine and reshape into the image of His Son, but the key word was *"refine."*

He wanted to take what He created and make it better---higher quality. The things He removed or added to my life were always for my good, to make me the best version of the woman He designed me to be. He didn't want to destroy me or squash my potential, but He wanted to refine it to produce even more life and health and peace.

Peace. There was a new word for me. Yet, as I stopped seeing my Heavenly Father through my earthly father's eyes, I was able to find peace.

I didn't have to work so hard for approval because God already approved of me.

As I learned to rest in His approval, I found that not only was I okay with myself, but I actually liked myself. It was okay to be who I was created to me---a driven, capable, funny, smart, opinionated woman of God who wants to make a difference in the world.

Yes, even though the time spent on overcoming my past wasn't on my agenda, it was THE BEST thing that could have happened in the lives of my mom, my brother, and I. The reason I'm writing this chapter and sharing all of these things isn't to make myself look good or to make my dad look bad. Rather, I'm hoping that sharing this part of my life will help you make the same choice that I made to allow God to take you through the process of facing and overcoming your past.

I understand that the term *"past"* doesn't mean the same for everyone. While I had to deal with my dad's abuse, your past may involve pain or damage from an adult other than your parents. Maybe there was a grandparent who treated you badly or constantly demeaned you. Perhaps it was a teacher.

Years ago I knew a lady who dreamed of being teacher. She loved kids and wanted to help them. However, the first obstacle she had to overcome was her own memory of a female teacher telling her she was stupid. This teacher was so mean to her, that my friend was afraid to go to college to make her dream come true. Although she did eventually overcome her fears, it was a real battle for her to overcome the voice of a mean, critical teacher from long ago.

Of course, the term *"past"* doesn't always have to involve your childhood. There are women who are carrying around the wounds and scars from old boyfriends or former husbands. It would be great if all romances ended in *"happily ever after,"* but they don't. We live in a world where there are men who haven't dealt with their own issues; rather, they take their pain and frustration out on the women in their lives.

Sometimes the result is physical abuse. Other times the abuse is verbal and emotional. Don't kid yourself, verbal and emotional abuse can be just as painful as physical abuse, because rather than attacking your body, the abuser is attacking your mind, your personality, your spirit. He is injuring the very essence of who you are.

Even after the relationship is over, many woman still struggle with wondering, *"Was he right about me?" "Am I the problem?" "Was I as stupid as he said I was?"* This is only a small illustration of the thoughts and questions that go through a woman's mind after she has been mistreated by someone that she loves.

The good news is that we have a God Who specializes in healing and deliverance. There is nothing He wants more than to heal the damage in your soul. One by one, He wants to heal your memories, heal the damage done to your heart, and help you overcome your past and become the woman He wants you to be.

However, He cannot begin this process until you give Him permission. This is where, once again, you are faced with a choice.

Do you want to continue living in the pain of the past or do you want to be free?

The good news is that we have a God Who specializes in healing and deliverance. There is nothing He wants more than to heal the damage in your soul.

Are you willing to face the past and bury it once and for all so that it stops damaging your future?

Will you allow God the time necessary to take you through this process, believing that everything He does is for your good?

I have to admit that when I first started going through the healing process, I hoped God would hurry up. I even prayed that He get it over with quickly so that I could get back to my life.

However, God wasn't so concerned about me getting back to my old life or even it hurrying up to get to the things I wanted out of life. Instead, He wanted me to start living life abundantly---free from the bondage and burdens that were controlling me.

Free to live a life of joy and peace fulfilling His purposes for my life.

As John 10:10 says, Jesus didn't come just to help us survive life; He came to give us abundant life.

The road to abundant life begins as we once again pass through the on-ramp of choosing to surrender and begin the journey of choosing to let God do whatever He needs to do to help us face our past and overcome our past knowing that the ultimate destination will lead to health, wholeness, peace, joy, and finding our true identity in Him.

Will you choose to allow God to help you face your past and overcome it?

Study Questions:

1. Are there things in your past that are keeping you in bondage---preventing you from becoming the woman you'd like to be?

2. Has your identity been distorted by another person's words, behaviors or ideas of "*how you should be*"?

3. Do you want to continue living in the pain of the past, or do you want to be free?

4. How do you feel about taking time out of your life to focus on overcoming your past?

5. Are you willing to face the past and bury it once and for all so that it stops damaging your future?

6. Will you allow God the time necessary to take you through this process, believing that everything He does is for your good?

7. What pro-active steps do you need to take to help you overcome your past? Do you need to spend time with God, visit a counselor, or learn new behavioral patterns?

*If you'd like to learn more about the Biblical principles for discovering complete healing and wholeness in your life, I encourage you to read my book, *Finding Healing*.

Chapter 7

UNIQUELY DESIGNED

Can I tell you a secret?

I do not like the ballet....or the opera.....or the symphony. Please do not be offended if you love these things. I just do not.

Here's another secret: for years of my life I pretended I loved these things because I thought I should.

I was seventeen years old the first time I went to the ballet. I remembering being so excited! Absolutely sure that I would love it, I put on my best dress and headed off for a night of sophistication and culture. I remember sitting in my chair preparing to be elated by the beauty I was about to see.

Instead, I was in for a surprise. Turns out, I don't really like the ballet. Honestly, it was one of the most boring nights I've ever spent, and I couldn't wait to go home. I remember walking around during intermission thinking, *"I wish this was over."*

The only thing was that even though I was genuinely bored, I didn't let anyone know this was how I was feeling. Instead, I acted like it was the best night of my life. I pretended that I loved it, that I thought it was beautiful and couldn't wait to go again.

Even when the people I was with started to say they were bored, I maintained that I was thrilled so that it would look like I had a more refined taste than I actually did. I didn't want anyone to actually know the truth—-that I was just a country girl who would have preferred a DC Talk concert over the ballet.

I followed the same pattern in music appreciation class when we were studying classical music. I tried so hard to like it! I'd close my eyes and tried really hard to concentrate on the music. I'd even try to picture someone figure skating to it (because I love figure skating). Yet, nothing worked. Deep inside, I knew I didn't like it. I like modern music with powerful words.

Still, once again, I pretended that I was entranced. Even when my friends complained about being forced to listen to concertos at 7:30 a.m., I maintained that I enjoyed it. After all, don't all sophisticated, cultured people love classical music?

Since that's who I wanted to be, I pretended the music was exhilarating and I was totally into it.

Of course, I didn't just play this game when it came to matters of culture.

Unfortunately, the need to pretend to be something I wasn't permeated too many areas of my life.

Looking back now, I can see it was a generational pattern. I come from a long line of people who carried a great deal of shame about different areas of their lives. To cover up their shame, they pretended.

They pretended that real life events didn't happen. They put on airs that they were more than they were. They basically lied about who they were and what their lives were like so that others would be impressed, but, even more so, that they would feel better about themselves.

You cannot fulfill God's plan or purpose for your life if you are pretending to be someone or something that you are not.

Even though I didn't find out until my twenties, my dad lived this way throughout his life. From the first day he met my mom, he told stories about himself, his family, his friends, and really every part of his life that weren't true. He maintained his cover and shared *"his stories"* throughout their marriage and the entire time my brother and I were growing up. It wasn't until I was back home from college that the Holy Spirit said *"enough!"* and started revealing the truth so that our whole family could be set free.

In the meantime, I picked up this pattern and adopted this generational iniquity in my life. Thankfully, I did not have as many tragedies to cover up in my life as he did.

What I did have was a lot of insecurities and a desire to have people like me. That's how this generational iniquity worked in my life.

By the time I graduated from college, it was a big problem that the Holy Spirit needed to address, so that I could repent, change, and allow Him to make me who He wanted me to be. Because here's the truth: You cannot fulfill God's plan or purpose for your life if you are pretending to be someone or something that you are not.

It's just not possible.

The truth is that God created you the way that you are for a purpose. You are the way you are for a reason. No part of your personality, your abilities, your tastes or even your physical qualities are a mistake. You are uniquely designed to fulfill God's plan for your life.

Whenever you pretend to be something that you are not or allow yourself to become a chameleon blending into the circumstances around you, you are basically telling God that He did something wrong when He created you.

You are also lying.

This was a truth that I had to face almost immediately after the truth about my dad's life began to be revealed. You see, up until this point, I didn't really think that what I was doing was that big of a deal. I mean, who cared if I said that I preferred peanut butter to chocolate just so a guy (who loved peanut butter) would like me? Did it really matter?

So what if I pretended to like football and even said I'd watched a game (even though I really watched the highlight reel in the morning so I'd have something to talk about)? Didn't all girls do this?

Did it really matter if I pretended that I had more experience, that my life was more exciting, or that I could identify with what my friends were talking about when my life was really so boring that I had no idea?

Who would it hurt if I pretended to love the humor of a popular late night talk show host (that I really didn't understand) or act like I was familiar with all of the high-end fashion designers when my idea of high-end was shopping at the Dress Barn?

Did these things really matter? It wasn't as if any of these things were important!

I just wanted to fit in, to make myself more interesting, more sophisticated, more appealing than I actually am.

Did it really matter if I didn't like the ballet?

For most of my high school and college life, I convinced myself that it didn't matter. Just move on, no big deal. Then we found out the truth about my dad.

Suddenly, I realized that it was an ENORMOUS deal. It was HUGE!

It was as if someone turned a huge spotlight on this generational pattern and showed me that it wasn't just about chocolate or football or the ballet. It was choosing to live a lie. I wasn't just pretending; I was giving ground to a destructive sin that caused so much pain and heartache in my family. As I experienced the incredible pain that this sin caused in my life and the life of my family, I prayed, *"I want this out of my life now."*

It was a prayer the Holy Spirit was more than willing to begin answering immediately.

The first thing I had to do was repent of the sin of lying.

I know, it sounds strange. Most of us look at *"altering the truth"* to fit in as an identity or self esteem issue. And it is. However, before we can deal with these issues we have to address the issue of the sin of lying and the results of giving it a place in our lives.

Proverbs 12:22 says, **"The Lord detests lying lips, but he delights in people who are trustworthy." (New International Version).**

Psalm 101:7 goes even further and says, **"No one who practices deceit will dwell in my house; no one who speaks falsely will stand in my presence."**

If that's not enough, we see that Revelations 21:8-9 lists liars with the *"big sinners"* - murderers, the sexually immoral, witches, and idol worshippers. It specifies, **"But the cowardly, the unbelieving, the vile, the murderers, the sexually immoral, those who practice magic arts, the idolaters and all liars—they will be consigned to the fiery lake of burning sulfur. This is the second death."**

As you can see, God takes lying very seriously. We need to take it seriously as well. This means we need to thoroughly repent, ask God to forgive us, and choose to stop doing it. Personally for me, this meant making a list of every time I could remember lying about who I was or what I liked. Given it was a twenty year pattern in my life, the list was pretty long. And yet, if you are serious about getting this sin out of your life, I'd encourage you to make the list. It really helped me to see that this pattern was a big deal in my life. By thoroughly repenting, I was able to thoroughly destroy this stronghold in my life and really determine that I was ready for a change.

The next thing I did was pray a prayer of spiritual deliverance so that no generational iniquities of lying could stay in my life. I know the term "spiritual deliverance" tends to make people nervous, but it doesn't really need to be this way. The truth is that, as a child of God, you need to engage in spiritual warfare. We all have things in our life that have been passed on to us from the generations gone by.

Whenever one of these things comes up, we need to use

the authority we are given in the name of Jesus and through His blood to pray and tell these things that they cannot stay in our lives any longer.

Here's a sample prayer:

"Heavenly Father, I want to belong totally to You. I give You my body, soul, and spirit. I want You to reign supreme in every area of my life.

I thank You, Lord Jesus, for dying on the cross for me. Please forgive me of every sin I have committed from birth until now. Put every sin underneath Your blood.

Forgive me for every time I've lied or pretended I was something that I was not. Lord Jesus, forgive me if, through these sinful acts, I have given ground to any generational iniquities.

I now take back all ground I have given to any spirit of Satan in the area of lying.

I take back all ground my forefathers may have given to Satan.

I command all spirits of Satan that are trying to attack me or oppress me to stop right now, to leave me right now and go into the pit forever because I now belong to Jesus Christ. You have no legal right to me anymore.

I invite you, Holy Spirit, to come into my life and fill every part of my being with Yourself.

Give me the fruit of the Spirit, and give me those gifts of the Spirit You desire me to have.

May your power, blessed Holy Spirit, flow through me, so that I may be a strong witness for the Lord Jesus Christ.

In Jesus' name, Amen.[1]"

After addressing the sin angle and removing the power that any generational iniquities had on my life, the next thing I had to do was get to the root of the problem.

Why did I feel the need to pretend to be something I was not?

Honestly, this question took a little more time to answer. And yet, the Holy Spirit was faithful.

During times of prayer, He showed me the root of my problems. Because while the tendency to pretend to be something I was not was generational, there were issues in my heart that caused me to choose this path. Together, we walked through my feelings of insecurity, my desires to not just be liked but admired, my fear of failure and shame, and my even deeper fear that if I wasn't more than I was than I wouldn't be loved. One by one I had to remember times when I felt *"less than,"* words spoken to me that made me think I wasn't enough, times I was made fun of, and even television shows and movies that influenced my thinking and made me feel bad about myself. As I walked with the Holy Spirit through each of these memories and preconceived ideas, I was able to find healing.

Of course, it wasn't enough just to get to the root of the problem. As with any healing work that God wants to do inside of your heart, you need to go forward into the next step and begin replacing lies with truth. For me, this meant studying the Bible and finding out what God really had to say about me.

One of the biggest truths that I had to not only hear, but let sink deep into my heart, was that God created me just the way I am for a unique purpose. This truth was a powerful key to unlocking my insecurities.

This is a truth that every person needs to know: From the day you were born, God created you with a unique plan and purpose in mind.

> **"For we are God's handiwork, created in Christ Jesus to do good works, which God prepared in advance for us to do." (Ephesians 2:10).**

One of the important truths found in this verse is that God created you the way that you are so that you could do what He wants you to do.

So often we miss this truth trying to cover up or hide the things we don't think are the best parts of ourselves. And yet, the truth is that those may be the exact things that God placed in our lives so that we could fulfill our purpose.

Here's another truth: From the moment of your conception, God has been watching you. In your mother's womb, before your mother even knew that she was pregnant, God was knitting you together. God created you just the way you are—-every unique detail.

As it says in Psalm 139:13-18:

> **You made all the delicate, inner parts of my body and knit me together in my mother's womb.**
>
> **Thank you for making me so wonderfully complex!**
>
> **Your workmanship is marvelous—how well I know it.**
>
> **You watched me as I was being formed in utter seclusion, as I was woven together in the dark of the womb.**

You saw me before I was born.

Every day of my life was recorded in your book.

Every moment was laid out

before a single day had passed.

How precious are your thoughts about me, O God.

They cannot be numbered!

I can't even count them;

they outnumber the grains of sand.

(New Living Translation).

No matter what you've heard, you are not a mistake. You are the way you are because God created you that way. This includes the things that you do or do not like about yourself. All of it was designed with a purpose in mind.

No matter what you've heard, you are not a mistake.

I remember being a young child and hearing a story of Amy Carmichael[2], a missionary to India in the early to mid 1900's. According to the story, when she was a little girl she was very unhappy with the color of her hair and eyes. Often she prayed, *"God, why couldn't You make me beautiful with blue eyes and blond hair?"* Yet, what she didn't know as a child was that the eye color and hair color that God gave her was exactly what she needed to fit into the Indian culture and minister to countless woman and children.

Even though I heard this story as a young girl, it wasn't until I was much older that it's truth really found a home in my heart.

Each of us is designed for a destiny. Rather than trying to hide who I was or pretend to be someone I was not, I would only begin to experience true fulfillment as I learned why God created me the way I am and began embracing it.

Another truth that I had to learn is that you can't fulfill your purpose as long as you are trying to copy someone else.

This was a big problem in my life, especially after I met my favorite pastors and decided that I wanted my life to be just like their lives.

Because even though they were great role models in many areas, God didn't intend my life to follow the exact same path that He led them to follow. He gave them different talents, tastes, and abilities so that they could carry the message He gave them and reach the people He wanted them to reach. However, He had a different audience for me and a different way of carrying the message. Although it sounds trite and cliche, God didn't need a carbon copy of them—-He needed me to be who He created me to be.

This is a truth that you need to grab hold of if you really want to find God's will for your life: *You weren't meant to copy other people. You need to be yourself.*

God's will is for you to be you. Now, granted He will always be working on your heart, refining you, and causing you to grow in Him. However, the essential material of who you are—-your personality, your story, your basic DNA will always be unique to you. Whenever you try to change it, distort it, hide it, or pretend that it is different, you are fighting a losing battle.

One of the things that has really helped me on my own journey to finding my purpose is learning more about my personality so that I could accept it. For instance, over the years I've learned that my personality is melancholy/chloric. I've also taken the Myer's Briggs personality test and learned that I am an ENFJ (although I honestly think I lean more toward INFJ). I've also studied and learned where my spiritual gifts lie.

Learning these things about myself has helped me to understand myself better. Through understanding, I've learned to be more accepting of myself.

However, the biggest step that I've taken to finding my passion, place, and purpose didn't come from a test. It came from simply being honest about who I am to myself and to others. For me, true freedom came as I took the bold step of just being real on a daily basis.

Trust me, this was not always easy for someone who was obsessed with keeping up appearances. And yet, there was also a bit of adventure in taking a chance and allowing myself to be seen, warts and all.

It came through being honest and admitting things like, "*I don't really like the ballet…or opera…or British television..I have an odd sarcastic sense of humor that people may or may not get….I would rather be at home watching television in my pajamas than be at a fancy event"* that helped me overcome.

One thing that really moved the ball forward on accepting myself was being vulnerable about my mistakes. When I started telling people or even writing about all of the stupid things that I do or that happen to me on a regular basis, it helped balance out my need to appear perfect all of the time.

And then of course, there was the choice to be honest about my life. At first, this was really hard for me because I was actually carrying a lot of my own shame about the path

God had taken my life on. Let's be honest, my story never has and still doesn't fit into a pretty little box.

And yet, an amazing thing happened as I began honestly and openly sharing my truth. People began to relate. Others who had similar stories or were experiencing the same feelings began finding hope and encouragement through my openness about my mess. Rather than people rejecting me, what I found was that the more real I was, the more they could relate. More importantly, the more I allowed myself to simply be who God created, the more He could use me to share His hope and healing with others.

It's funny—-I spent so many years trying to make myself into someone with an important purpose. Yet it wasn't until I decided to be the most honest version of myself that I was able to fulfill God's plan for my life.

The same is true for all of us.

We can only discover our true purpose and passion when we are bold enough to be ourselves.

When we stop pretending, putting up facades or trying to be someone else we are able to fulfill the amazing plans God has for our lives.

We can only discover our true purpose and passion when we are bold enough to be ourselves.

When we give up fighting God's design and instead embrace His design, we find that He created us exactly the way we need to be to do what He has called us to do.

Study Questions:

1. Have you ever pretended to be different than you are to impress people or make yourself feel better?

2. Do you think this is normal or something we need to overcome?

3. Do you believe that pretending to be someone who you are not is lying?

4. How do you feel about the idea that pretending to be someone who you are not could be passed down from generation to generation? Can you identify this pattern in your life? What caused your ancestors to feel they needed to pretend? Is this the same reason you feel the need to pretend?

5. If you do not see a generational pattern in your life, what do you think is the root cause of your need to pretend to be something you're not?

6. This chapter says, *"No matter what you've heard, you are not a mistake. You are the way you are because God created you that way. This includes the things that you do or do not like about yourself. All of it was designed with a purpose in mind."* How does this make you feel about yourself and your purpose?

7. How can accepting the unique way that God created you help you find your passion, your place, and your purpose?

8. What practical steps can you take to stop being fake and start being the real you?

9. Do you like the ballet? (Okay, that was just meant to be a joke!)

Chapter 8

LOVING YOUR REAL LIFE

Most of my life, I've lived fairly close to the sweetest place on earth---Hershey, Pennsylvania. I grew up going to Hersheypark, seeing the street lights shaped as Hershey kisses as I drove through the town and breathing in the amazing smell of chocolate. Still, I have to admit that whenever I hear someone excited to be taking a trip to Hershey or even see it offered as a destination prize on a game show, I think, *"Really?? Hershey??"*

I mean it's a great place, but having been there a thousand times, it's not that big of a deal. I feel the same way whenever I'm in town and see a tourist taking a picture of a rollercoaster at Hersheypark. Again, I find myself chuckling and thinking, *"Dude, it's a rollercoaster---at Hersheypark---it's not like it's Mt. Rushmore. No pictures necessary."*

The truth is that my familiarity with the area has caused this vacation destination to lose some of its allure. Of course,

I'm on the other side of the equation whenever I hear one of my friends who lives near the beach say, *"I just want to get away to the mountains."* That's when I think, *"Really??? You live at the best place on earth, why would you ever want to leave?"*

We often miss the beauty and potential of the situations and circumstances with which we are the most familiar.

That's the problem with the familiar. Just like Hersheypark has lost some of it's magic for me over the years and my friends too often only see crowds and traffic at the beach, we often miss the beauty and potential of the situations and circumstances with which we are the most familiar.

This isn't just true of vacation spots, it's also a very common life problem. I see it over and over again....people who are so busy dreaming about their future purpose that they completely overlook the purposes they are destined to fulfill in their current situations.

For instance, the other day my friend was telling me about a woman she knew who was completely obsessed with finding the ultimate ministry position. She called it her *"sweet spot."* Unfortunately, while she was waiting for her *"someday"* to come, she was completely missing her ability to make her here-and-now the sweetest place on earth.

I'll admit that I've been there.

As I've told you before, in my early adult life I spent way too much time waiting for God to open doors for the next big thing. I had big dreams of what my life would be like someday...when I was married...when I had kids...when I had a home of my own... when I finally had the ministry position I thought I deserved (insert major eye roll here). One of the lessons that the Holy Spirit had to teach me was that it was wrong to waste my days dreaming of the days to come while I ignored my purpose in the here and now.

The truth was that I wasn't called to just wait….I was called to occupy. God's purpose for my life at this time was to…

….Grow in my relationship with Jesus

….Allow the Holy Spirit to heal my heart from my past

….Love my parents and my brother

…..Learn all that I could

…..Serve my family by helping my mom and brother with their physical issues and taking care of the house God provided (even if it was my parent's home).

Most importantly, this was the time in my life when I learned that my calling is to love Jesus and fulfill the purpose He's given me in every season and circumstance in my life. It was here that I learned that every season of life has a purpose, and my purpose is to fulfill my role right now wherever God has placed me.

But trust me when I say that I did not come to this place overnight. (Sorry, that's just not me). Instead, it took time. When God first started leading me on this journey, I didn't understand it at all. Instead, I wasted so much time trying to knock down doors of opportunity—-searching for anyone or anything that would get me out of the place that God had me and put me back on the road to making my dreams come true.

Sometimes I look back on those earliest days and feel sorry for my family who had to live with me. I was so sulky!!

Caught in a pity party, I thought about myself and my circumstances far too much. I was difficult, depressed, and somedays just plain pitiful.

Thankfully, neither the Holy Spirit or my mom put up with this attitude for very long! One day, around Christmastime, while I was having a pity party during my prayer time (basically whining about how much better the holidays would be if I had a husband, kids, and a home of my own), the Holy Spirit spoke to me. Although these weren't His exact words, He essentially said, *"Stop! Enough with the pity party! Stop feeling sorry for yourself for all that you don't have and start enjoying what I have given you. Enjoy this Christmas with your family. Spend time with your mom. Decorate the home you're living in. Stop wishing you were somewhere else and fully embrace and enjoy where you are."*

I remember that day being a turning point for me. Starting that Christmas, I began making a focused effort to stop living my life for what might someday be, and start finding my purpose in what God had presently given me. Honestly, looking back, this was one of the best decisions I've ever made in my life.

You see, what I didn't know then was that there would be a fifteen-year gap between the day I graduated from college and when I went into full-time ministry. As of today, I am still single and living with my brother in the house where we grew up. So obviously, it took quite a while to get even some of the things I was dreaming of and some—well, they may never happen. And yet, because of the choice that I made years ago to stop focusing on someday and choose to live with contentment in each and every circumstance in which God has placed me, I have found joy, peace, and fulfillment in my life.

When I finally got over my quest for the next big thing, I

found that there are so many treasures in the little things that we take for granted. I found the joy in ordinary days. I've experienced the deepest love that comes from relationships with family and friends, and I've found the incredible fulfillment that comes from a life of serving God and others.

Today, I cringe when I think how much I would have missed had I not made the choice in my early twenties to choose to enjoy my real life by embracing contentment. I'm so glad I made a different choice.

Years ago I heard a quote that said, *"Life may not be the party we hoped for, but while we're here we should dance."*

In Philippians 4:11-13 Paul says it this way, **"For I have learned to be content whatever the circumstances." (New International Version).**

In their own way, they are both saying the same thing---this is the life God has chosen to give me, I might as well enjoy it.

I'm not going to say that this is always easy. The truth is that it's hard to take a *"que sara sara"* (whatever will be will be) attitude when your life isn't going the way you hoped or dreamed.

I'm sure that Paul understood this. Think about where he was when he wrote these words. He was sitting in prison for committing no crime other than preaching about Jesus. I'm sure there were days that he longed to feel the sun on his face, to take a walk wherever he wanted, or to eat better food than he was given.

However, as Paul sat in prison he had two choices: he could wallow in self-pity and become bitter or he could choose to be content and accept that God was allowing this in his life. He could waste his days wishing he weren't in jail, or he could use his time to write letters and encourage the churches. Paul's choice was to learn to be content.

This is a key phrase: Paul learned to be content.

He taught his thoughts and his emotions to accept that this was God's will for his life.

Contentment is something we have to force ourselves to "put on."

He learned to stop focusing on what he wished his circumstances were, and to start making the most of each day in his circumstances.

This is a vital lesson for any one who wants to follow God's will for their life. You need to accept that God has specifically placed you where you are, at this time in your life. Rather than wasting time feeling sorry for yourself, pouting, and punishing the world because you are unhappy, you need to accept God's plan and learn to be content where He's placed you.

Trust me, this is something you will have to teach yourself.

It's not going to come naturally. Contentment is something we have to force ourselves to *"put on."*

It's like getting up and getting dressed in the morning. Speaking only for myself, I can say that I look very different when I first get out of bed in the morning than I do when I leave the house. Quite frankly, my early morning self is not attractive.

When I first get up, my hair is a mess; there are pillow marks on my face and sleepy eye gunk around my eyes. If I decided to go through my day looking like I did first thing in the morning, I think I'd turn a few heads. (Not in a good way, but more like, *"Can you believe she left the house looking like that?"*)

Obviously, I make another choice.

I get up, wash my hair, brush my teeth, and make myself look better. Then I *"put on"* makeup, clean clothes, some jewelry, and choose how I'm going to look before I leave the house.

Trust me, my choice to *"put on"* better attire, makes all the difference.

Just like my decision to put my *"sleepy time attire"* aside for the day and make myself more presentable to the world makes all the difference in my outward appearance, so our choice to *"put on"* contentment will make all the difference in our inner wellbeing.

Even though it may be more natural for us to wear an attitude of discontentment, jealousy, anger or depression, choosing this road will ultimately lead us to a place that we don't want to go: The Pit of Self-Pity. There are no happy or fulfilled citizens in that town---just sad, disgruntled malcontents wallowing in their own anger that things didn't turn out the way they wanted. What a tragedy!

The good news is that this does not have to be the end of any woman's story. We were not created to live our lives in the Pit of Self-Pity. God has a much higher purpose in mind for each of His daughters. Whether or not we fulfill God's purpose for our lives or waste our lives in the Pit of Self-Pity depends on the choices we make.

Will we choose surrender or selfishness? Will we choose contentment or self-pity? The choice is up to you.

At this point you may be saying, *"Okay, I hear you, and I want to make positive choices. I want to put on contentment; I just don't know where to start."*

Here are some practical steps to start teaching yourself to be content:

Stop focusing on what you want and thank God for what you have.

Thessalonians 5:18, **"Be thankful in all circumstances, for this is God's will for you who belong to Christ Jesus." (New Living Translation).**

When we focus on what we have to be thankful for, it changes our perspective and helps us become more content. It may sound old-fashioned and corny, but there really is something to be said for *"counting your blessings"* as a way of changing your attitude.

As I said before, this was something I had to determine to do in my life. Rather than wishing I had a home of my own, I had to thank God for all of the comforts He provided in my parent's home and learn to love and treat this home the way I would my own. Instead of wishing for a husband and family, I learned to thank God for my family and treasure each moment that I spent with my mom and brother. Rather than wishing for my dream job, I taught myself to enjoy each responsibility that God gave me each day and find true pleasure and accomplishment in each one. In every circumstance I had to focus not on what I wish I had, but on what God provided and enjoy it.

Choose to Praise God

One of the things I had to learn on my journey to loving my real life was that I had to turn off some of the outside influences that were creating appetites in my life that could not be filled. To help me choose contentment meant I had to turn off some of the television shows I was watching, stop reading all secular magazines and romance novels, and say *"goodbye"* to secular music. Instead, I had to find other more positive influences that would encourage me to keep following the plan that God had for my life.

One of the best ways to do this is to put on some praise music and start singing along. Put on the garment of praise to replace your spirit of heaviness. (Isaiah 61:3) Follow Paul's example and choose to praise the Lord even in the most difficult of circumstances, and watch your attitude change!

Focus on Being a Blessing to Someone Else

Nothing will change your attitude and help you experience contentment more than taking your eyes off of your own situation and reaching out to help someone else.

This was a big part of my story. You see, even though when I first came home from college I was being mentored by my mom, as the years went on and both she and my brother began developing physical issues, they needed help from me. During those years, my purpose was helping them and taking care of our home.

The truth is that there really is no better way to get your eyes off of yourself than to find your purpose in helping someone else. It's just so meaningful! For me, it was during this time that I prayed (and genuinely meant it), *"God, if this is all that I do for the rest of my life...loving You and serving my family...then I'm good with that."*

Accepting that God Knows Best

Okay, I'm not going to minimize this---I know that some of you are dealing with really difficult situations where it is really hard to be content. You're suffering and you want out of these circumstances NOW. How can you learn to be content?

Let's look at Psalm 131 and take a lesson from King David---a man who was very familiar with heartache and difficult circumstances. It reads:

> **My heart is not proud, Lord, my eyes are not haughty;**
>
> **I do not concern myself with great matters or things too wonderful for me.**
>
> **But I have calmed and quieted myself; I am like a weaned child with its mother; like a weaned child I am content.**
>
> **Israel, put your hope in the Lord both now and forevermore. (New International Version).**

Very much like the Apostle Paul, David knew that the key to being content was to be calm and accept the circumstances, quiet his soul, and put his hope in the Lord. He had fully submitted his will to God's will and relinquished the "*I deserves*" that come with a proud heart and the discontentment that comes with an envious heart. Instead, he chose to be humble and trust that God knew what He was doing and that he would be content to live in God's will for his life.

Believe me when I say, I know this is not easy. As I said, I spent too many days choosing the wrong road and being discontent with the path God chose for my life. I wanted more. I thought I deserved more, and I envied those who had more.

Then the Holy Spirit convicted me of the sin of discontentment. He showed me that I had to stop envying other people's lives and begin enjoying and appreciating my own life. During that time I had to learn, like David, to quiet my soul and learn to be content.

At first, it wasn't easy. It never is when we're retraining our minds. However, looking back now I can honestly say that this *"correction"* was one of the greatest gifts God has ever given me because it taught me how to put on contentment.

Now when I'm feeling the pull toward discontentment or depression, I've learned that it's my responsibility to make a choice, take action, and put on contentment.

Whenever I choose to follow Paul's footsteps and choose contentment, I can genuinely say that when the moment of temptation passes and I'm thinking clearly again, I am happy with what God has provided. I have learned that whatever God gives and where ever He leads, it's going to be pretty wonderful. Maybe not exactly what I planned, but still pretty wonderful.

Contentment is believing that God has a purpose in every season and then living out each moment in that season with passion.

So what about you?

There are choices standing before you: Contentment or Discontentment, Joy or Envy, Thankfulness or Ungratefulness. Which one will you choose?

Will you follow the path that leads to the Pit of Self-Pity or will you choose to take the road less travelled and choose to fulfill the purpose God has for your life?

The choice is completely dependent on whether or not you will learn to be content.

"Contentment is believing that God has a purpose in every season and then living out each moment in that season with passion."

I love this statement because it really sums up the connection between contentment and finding your passion, your place, and your purpose. It reminds us that God is in control of every situation. As it says in Psalm 139:16, God has every day of your life mapped out. Whenever we are following God's plan for our lives, no day or period of time is wasted.

You are the only one who can choose to waste a season in your life by refusing to thoroughly embrace the plan that God has for every moment of your life.

Today, I am so thankful for the day that the Holy Spirit said, *"Enough. Stop daydreaming, pouting, and looking for the next big thing and learn to love your real life."*

I'm even more thankful that I chose to follow His direction. I'm so glad that I chose not only to endure those days, but to also enjoy them. In reflection, I can see now that some of those moments were the most precious memories in my life.

Looking back on my life, I'm so glad that my memories aren't filled with days spent pouting or wishing I had a different life. Instead, I remember intimate moments spent with Jesus and precious times spent with family.

I remember dancing with my mom in a department store when a favorite song played.

I remember late night conversations filled with tears and other evenings filled with roars of laughter.

I recall days filled with projects, remodeling, learning to landscape, and working hard alongside my family. I remember the exhaustion, but also the sense of accomplishment at the end of a long day.

Most of all, I remember the times when God moved in our

lives. When the God of the Universe stepped into the lives of a tiny little family that no one noticed and moved mountains and performed miracles.

Was it the life I always imagined? No.

Was it always easy?

Honestly, no. There were days that were extremely difficult when the Holy Spirit was revealing my dad's truth and my dad was responding in negative ways.

Yet even through these difficulties, I can honestly say that this was one of the richest, most fulfilling times in my life. It was here that I found that my true purpose was having a relationship with Jesus and serving Him, that my place was loving and being loved by the people in my life, and where I discovered that my passion was helping women find hope and healing in Jesus.

Yes, I am so happy that I obeyed the Holy Spirit and chose to find contentment and enjoy the real life He gave me rather than spend my days imagining a better life.

Today, I hope that this chapter will help you to make the same choice.

Again, you are probably not living in the exact same situation as me. However, I know that there are people reading this who are working at a job they don't love. There are others that God has placed in a time of *"waiting"* who are wondering, *"When is God going to give me new direction?"* The truth is that no matter what your exact circumstances, the heart of the issue is the same. You're wondering, *"When is God going to give me the life I really want?"*

Today, I want to encourage you to follow the pattern of David and Paul and take a rest from asking that question.

Instead, choose to quiet your soul and begin focusing on enjoying the life God has given you right now.

I can promise you that even if you can't see it, He has a purpose in this season in your life. Tomorrow may or may not be what you expect, but you can choose to make today amazing.

Right now I want to encourage you to pray this prayer and then spend some time with Jesus reflecting on ways that you can make the most of the real life He has given you.

Ask Him to show you how you've been indulging the sins of self-pity and envy and repent.

Then ask Him to show you specific ways that you can make the most of your circumstances today. Ask Him to help you to find your purpose, your place, and your God-breathed passions for today.

Finally, start enjoying and embracing the real life He's given you.

Today, you can make that choice. You can choose to enjoy every moment and find purpose in your real life.

Let's pray:

"Dear Heavenly Father, I come to you in Jesus' name and ask you to forgive me for every time that I have been discontented, each time I've chosen the road that leads to Self-Pity, and every time I've followed my natural inclinations of selfishness and been a poor reflection of a Christian.

Please help me to daily choose to put on contentment. Help me to lay down my will and, like Paul, learn to be content in every situation through the power of Jesus Christ. Amen."

Study Questions:

1. A quote in the chapter said, *"Life may not be the party we hoped for, but while you're here, we should dance."* How can you make this a part of your life?

2. How can we *"learn"* to be content?

3. What can we learn from David and Paul about finding contentment?

4. The chapter says, *"Contentment is believing that God has a purpose in every season and then living out each moment in that season with passion."* What does this mean to you?

5. Take a moment and reflect on this question: *What am I missing in my life while I'm waiting for something better?*

6. What are some specific choices you can make to help you *"put on"* contentment?

Chapter 9

YOUR PEOPLE ARE YOUR PURPOSE

The other day I was scrolling through Facebook when I saw a picture of a friend of mine holding her beautiful baby niece. Even though the picture was adorable, it was what she wrote that stayed in my mind. Above her post she wrote, *"This is my purpose…with her."*

Immediately I thought, *"Yes, she gets it!"*

You see, my friend has not yet married or had children. She is thriving in her career and making a dynamic difference in people's lives. Yet what really impresses me about her is that she has completely grasped the concept that her purpose is to thrive within her family unit. She realizes that a large part of her purpose in life is to love and serve her family---to be a daughter, a sister, a sister-in-law, and now an aunt.

I wish I'd been so wise when I was her age.

Unfortunately, I was not. Instead, I had some preconceived ideas that distorted my ability to understand that my people were my purpose. Once again, the Holy Spirit had to help me separate God's truth from the cultural concepts, so that I could surrender to His plan for my life and walk in the life He had for me.

You see, throughout my life I've understood that family is very important to God.

Genesis 2:18-19 shows us that God knew from the very beginning that it is not good for man (or woman) to be alone. That's why He created the institution of marriage and family —to fill the deep need inside of each human being for connection and relationship. Before there was work, community, countries, or even church, there was family.

In my early twenties, I understood this concept. My issue came with the narrow way that I defined family. As a young, single woman I thought that the only way to fulfill my purpose in this area of my life was to be married and have children of my own.

Rather than being like my friend, I pouted and sulked and wondered why God wasn't filling this essential need in my life.

I was completely wrong.

Now before I go any further, let me backtrack and make one thing very clear: I am a big believer and supporter of the institution of marriage and family. As I said, we see that God ordained marriage as a sacred institution in Genesis and He continued to bless it throughout the Bible. If you are blessed to be a wife and a mother, than I am so happy for you. I love my married friends and fully support the purpose that God has for their lives.

If you are a wife and mother, you already know that a large part of your purpose is loving and serving your family. Right after your relationship with God, this should be your top priority. The Bible provides so much teaching to help you strengthen your marriage and raise your children to be godly men and women. During this time in your life, one of your purposes is to learn all that God has to say about marriage and family and develop ways to apply His principles to your life.

It's very important that as a wife and mother, you take this responsibility seriously and truly understand that the people in your life are your purpose. One of the saddest stories I've ever observed was a friend who spent so much time obsessing over finding God's will for their life that they ignored their family. When God didn't lead them to the *"big position"* that they thought they deserved, they started treating their spouse and children abusively. In the end, they lost their family because they didn't understand that God's purpose for this season in their life was their family.

The same applies to married women and moms as I say to single women so often, don't waste this season in your life wishing you were somewhere else. I know somedays it seems like *"the dream"* isn't actually very dreamy at all as you face challenges and struggles, yet, this is still the calling that God has for your life.

Love your family. Be there for them. Give everything you have to fulfilling God's purpose to the people in your life. Make that your passion and watch as God blesses your efforts.

What if you are not a wife or mother?

This is a question that many women ask. In fact, in 2017,

45.2 percent of adults over the age of 18 were single.[1] Among this number are people who have never been married, those who are divorced, and those who are widowed. Even though most of these people will be married at some point in their lives, as a single woman myself, I believe it is important that we understand that even if we are going through a season of singleness, it is still God's will to fill the need that we all have in our lives for family.

This was a big part of my journey to finding my passion, my place, and my purpose.

As I mentioned before, after I came home from college, I moved into my parents' home. For years, my mom was there to serve as my mentor and teacher during the hardest times in my life. When I came home broken and in need of discipleship, she was there to share with me all she'd gone through on her spiritual journey and point me in the right direction. She taught me, inspired me, and challenged me on this very difficult road. The years of time and sacrifice she poured into Jamie and I and even our ministry showed a faith that was beyond what anyone could expect or imagine at the time. She was my friend, my support system, and my mentor all wrapped into one.

Still, as time went on, our relationship changed as we went from just her helping me to me helping her. When environmental allergies became a major issue in her life, I was then given the opportunity to be a blessing to her and offer her the support--- physical and emotional---that she needed.

It was around the time of Jamie's college graduation that she had her first major allergic episode. We'd purchased a used car and were driving home when her throat and tongue started to swell. We had to rush her to the doctor as she had an allergic reaction to the cleaning products they used to recondition the car. The smell was so strong and the allergy so aggressive that we eventually had to take the car back to the dealer and get a refund.

Meanwhile, Mom went to the doctor to see what was happening. Even though they ran tests and tried different cures, in the end, it was determined that she had environmental allergies and the only cure would be lifestyle adjustments. Day by day her allergies and the constant pain she lived with in her mouth and tongue became more and more of a controlling factor in her life.

Before long, she was allergic to any type of chemical smell---including most cleaning products. We very quickly became experts in natural cleaning solutions like baking soda and vinegar so that she would be safe in her own home. Even then, she couldn't really touch these products, so I took over cleaning the house.

When we couldn't find a natural solution, we had to be very careful to always stick to the same laundry detergents, dish washing liquid, and even body soap. Any alteration or even using too much of one of these products would cause swelling and potentially shut down her lungs. She was allergic to perfume, hairspray, and facial cleansers. Another big allergen was ink---she couldn't be around a freshly printed newspaper or magazine.

She had to be careful everywhere she went, and she really couldn't go anywhere alone for fear that she'd get into the wrong smell and her lungs would shut down. More and more, these allergies became an invisible disability that took over her and our lives. During this time, my life and my responsibilities consisted mostly of taking care of our home, helping Mom, and being alert for any allergens that might be potentially dangerous. I was a full-time caregiver.

The truth is that even though these days were hard (because I'm not going to lie, it is incredibly hard to watch someone you love suffer and to take care of them as they do), quite honestly, they were some of the best days of my life.

Even though these days had a much slower pace and were much quieter than my current life, they were extremely rich. They were filled with deep conversations, laughter and private jokes, finding ways to overcome obstacles together, and just being a family.

For these years in my life, I found my purpose and place serving my family. I absolutely loved it!

During this season of my life, I made a decision I will never regret. I decided to be at peace and enjoy my life.

I'm not exactly sure when it happened or how it happened, but I know there came a day when I really came to peace with God and said, *"If this is how You want me to serve You for the rest of my life---by serving my family---I'm ok with that. I love You and I love them, and I'm good."*

Here's the really amazing thing—-I meant it.

I loved spending time with my mom and Jamie. Together, the three of us had a blast!

I enjoyed taking care of our home, being domestic and learning new skills.

Maybe I enjoyed it more because I was doing so many of these things with my mom and I loved spending time with her. We cooked, gardened, took care of the house, went on short excursions in the car, listened to music, watched movies, talked and laughed and many times cried together.

The truth is that now when I look back on those days I

have to force myself to remember the allergies or the injuries. What I remember was the love---the closeness---the memories that we made.

It was through this experience that I learned that God created all of us—-married, single, widowed, or divorced—to be a part of a family. It's like my brother said when he was speaking to men on the topic of family: *"So often single people think they can ignore this teaching, but my question to you is, 'Were you hatched?' We all have families, and it is God's will that we all learn to function and thrive in those relationships."*

So how do we do this?

Start by asking yourself:

1. *Who are the members of my immediate family?* Stop right now and make a list:

2. Then place your role into these sentences: I am called to be a__________________ and ____________________ and ______________________.

For me, it looks like this: *"I am called to be a daughter and sister."*

A single mom could add *"mother"* to that list.

My friend can add *"aunt."*

What titles can you add? Perhaps granddaughter, grandmother or cousin.

The point is to make a list of the people in your family and realize the role you play in their lives.

3. Then ask yourself, *what steps can I take to fulfill my purpose in the lives of those God has given me?*

Ask yourself:

"Do I believe that my purpose is to make a difference in the lives of these people?"

"Have I ever thought about this before?"

"Am I fulfilling or ignoring this purpose in my life?"

"Do I need to make any changes to start fulfilling my purpose?

As someone who is living this principle in her own life, I can promise you that it is life-changing when you realize that your purpose is to love the people in your life. It will keep you from being alone and fill your life with purpose, fulfillment, and a tremendous amount of joy. I know, because even now, I am experiencing this in my life.

You see, even today as I'm writing this book, God has still not chosen marriage as a part of my story. However, even after my mom passed away and I no longer had the same responsibilities to care for her, I am still not alone.

Instead, I still live with my father and my brother. When God began opening doors for ministry, He arranged for my brother and I to work together as a team. What's funny is that I'm living the life I believed God called me to twenty years ago, only I'm not ministering alongside of a husband. Instead, my brother and I are traveling, ministering, and working side by side. Once again, I am learning that my place and purpose is alongside the family God has given me. Without them, I am unfulfilled, and they are incomplete without me.

Like my friend, I have finally realized that right here with my family....that is my purpose.

Of course, I know there are some of you who are saying, "*Nice thought, 'Des, very pie in the sky. But my family has issues…it's not always easy to play a role in their lives.*"

Well, first of all let me say that I completely understand. Because although I always had a great relationship with my mom, my relationship with my dad has always been difficult because of his choices. And yet, part of my life's purpose is showing God's love to my dad and shining God's light into His life.

Has this always been an easy purpose? No.

Still, it is part of my life's calling and purpose. As I have done my best to fulfill this purpose (not always totally successfully, but I've tried), the Holy Spirit has been able to move in both his life and mine in ways that I don't think would have happened if I'd have abandoned him after my mom died.

Just because someone is difficult doesn't mean you have no purpose in their lives---or they have none in yours.

One lesson I've learned is that just because someone is difficult doesn't mean you have no purpose in their lives---or they have none in yours. The truth is that family can be difficult, yet out of great difficulties, God can do great things.

Personally, I can't say exactly what that will look like for you, because only you know your exact situation. All I can say is consult the Holy Spirit, ask what purpose He wants you to play in a difficult person's life, and then obey.

Never close your heart to the possibility of forgiveness. Be open to talking, trying to mend a relationship and at the very least, finding peace within yourself that you did all that you could to mend a fence.

Even if the other person isn't willing to do the work to bring about healing, choose to be kind. Show them love and respect by sending a card on holidays, calling to wish them a Happy Birthday, and praying for them. Perhaps your purpose in their life is to demonstrate God's love and forgiveness even if a normal, healthy relationship isn't possible.

Truly ponder the words of Luke 6:32-36 and see how they apply to your situation.

> **"If you love those who love you, what credit is that to you?**
>
> **.....But love your enemies, do good to them, and lend to them without expecting to get anything back. Then your reward will be great, and you will be children of the Most High, because he is kind to the ungrateful and wicked.**
>
> **Be merciful, just as your Father is merciful." (New International Version).**

What do you do if you're truly at the point where you've tried everything to mend relationships with your family and they just aren't interested? Or what if you are among those who really don't have any family in their lives?

The good news is that God has supplied a way for you to still experience all of the benefits of family by being a part of His family—-His church. Just because you may not have a biological family to fill the need for family in your life, doesn't mean you have to be alone. Instead, your local church is filled with mothers, fathers, sisters, brothers, grandmas, grandpas, aunts, and uncles who want to be a part of your life. Even more importantly, they need you to be a part of their lives and fulfill the purpose God has for you in His family.

This was such an important truth for Jamie and I in the years following our mom's death. The truth was that back then, our relationship with our dad was really bad. We were trying to forgive, trying to be kind, but it was a daily struggle.

Even though we had each other, we still felt lonely. Yet, God did not allow us to stay that way. Instead, as we became involved in our local church, God began supplying people to fill some of the needs in our lives. Over the years, He's placed people in our lives who we love and trust just like family. People who are there for us no matter what and love us no matter what we are going through.

He also gave us opportunities to love.

One of my favorite examples of this was the opportunities we were given to serve in our local church's children's ministry department. I'm not sure who got more out of this experience —the kids or us. I had a blast playing with the 3 to 5 year olds on Wednesday nights, traveling with older kids to Junior Bible Quiz tournaments (which we never won, but we sure did enjoy the trip and McDonalds afterwards)! I loved the opportunity to teach a class of 3rd to 5th grade girls and pour everything I knew about being a godly woman into them. We had so much fun cooking, doing projects, and spending time together. It was honestly one of the greatest blessings of my life because it filled my need for family. I was able to give and receive love as a part of a community of believers and again found my passion, my place, and my purpose in meeting this need in their lives.

This is an important truth for all Christians, married, single, young, old, male or female: God has a place and purpose for you in His church. Whatever your stage in life, He wants you to seek Him and ask where that place is and how you can best serve His family. Then embrace His calling and do whatever He is asking you to do in this season with all of your heart, remembering that you aren't just volunteering for a job, you are loving and serving your family, God's family.

And don't be surprised if your place in God's family shifts and changes over the years. I've discovered that just as we grow and mature, God often changes our role in His family. This is something we need to allow Him to do. Because that's how family works—-it isn't stagnant, it's always growing, changing, adding new members and saying goodbye to others. Needs change, people change, and we need to be willing to move with the Holy Spirit's flow and always be open to whatever new role He is leading us to fill in His family.

Above all, remember that no one member of the family, no matter their role, is more valued or important than the other. Instead, it takes all of us finding our purpose and filling our place at the table for the family to function properly. (I Corinthians 12:12-31). You can't fill someone else's spot. Nope, we need you to be you!

Over the years, I have come to wholeheartedly believe this truth:

It is God's will for all of us to make the people in our lives our purpose.

It is God's will for all of us to make the people in our lives our purpose.

For many women, they fulfill this purpose through their roles as wives and mothers. And for other women, it is God's will for you to identify your role as an aunt, sister, daughter, niece, cousin, granddaughter, and find your God-Given purpose among your family.

Just as He said in Genesis, it is not good for humans to be alone.

Psalm 68:6 says, "**God places the lonely in**

families." (New Living Translation). Today I'm asking you:

Who is your family?

What role does God want you to play in their lives?

What can you do to find your place and purpose among the people God has put in your life?

You, too, can find the joy and contentment that my friend found when she said,

"This is my purpose....with my family."

Study Questions:

1. Who are the members of your immediate family?

2. Make a list of the people in your family and realize the role you play in their lives. Place your role into these sentences: I am called to be a ____________ and ______________ and______________.

3. Ask yourself, *"What steps can I take to fulfill my purpose in the lives of those God has given me?"*

4. Do you have family members who make it difficult to have a relationship with them? What are some practical steps you can take to fulfill your purpose in their lives?

5. After reading Luke 6:32-36, how do you think God wants you to respond to the difficult people in your life?

6. How can your church fill a role of family in your life?

7. Are you willing to open yourself up to fulfilling God's purpose within your church?

8. How has this chapter challenged you personally regarding making your people your purpose?

Chapter 10

DESIGNED TO SERVE

Several years ago a gentleman volunteered to help us with my brother's ministry, Mantour Ministries. We were happy for the help—after all, there's a lot to do and lots of boxes to carry as we set up a Mantour Conference. Before we accepted his help, we had a long discussion about what we needed and what would be expected of him.

Only I'm not sure he was listening because shortly after his first event he came to us and explained that he didn't believe God was calling him to do behind-the-scenes work. Going forward, he thought he should focus on the ministry that took place on the stage.

We were stunned. I mean, really, what did he think we were going to say? *"Alright, why don't you sit here and focus on your stage ministry, and all of the rest of us will carry boxes, set up tables and work behind the scenes."*

He didn't continue with us for much longer.

Looking back now, I think it's funny. The poor guy had so much to learn about life. As I remember myself at that age, I remember that I had many of the same ideas that had to go through a Holy Spirit adjustment.

As I said before, when I was young, I had a lot of ideas of what ministering would look like for me. I imagined wearing designer suits, jetting all over the country, and eating room service in fancy hotels as people filled arenas waiting to hear me speak.

What I never imagined was service. Like our volunteer, I was all about the stage time and thought someone else could take care of the set-up.

It's kind of ironic that now, when we do Mantour Conferences, my responsibilities are to manage behind the scenes, carry boxes, work registration and book tables, and make sure the speakers have all that they need. I've come a long way, baby! But it didn't happen overnight.

No, for me, learning to put on servanthood was a process. It started during my junior and senior year in college when I had my very first legitimate, paid ministry position at a Christian retreat. What was my big exciting job?

Well, it was a fancy one: kid's ministry and housekeeping. For the first month, it was mostly just housekeeping. Yep, I was the girl who cleaned the guest's bathrooms, made the beds, and took out the trash. (Not exactly the internship of my dreams.) And yet I knew that everybody had to pay their dues, so I thought, *"A few months of this and God will open bigger doors."*

Well, that's not exactly what happened. Instead, twelve months later God brought me back home after graduation where, after a few years of kicking and screaming and trying to find an *"important"* position, I finally settled into the the fact that once again my role was to serve. As I said in the last chapter, for years I found my place and purpose taking care of our home and helping my family. Once again, my main jobs were cleaning the bathroom, washing dishes, and doing laundry because with my mom's allergies, she simply couldn't. (After so many years of practice, I am really good at cleaning a toilet!)

Of course, I got to do lots of other things during this time. I learned to landscape when our yard went through a major issue with flooding. When our house started falling apart, we learned to drywall, paint, tear up floors, and even build on a laundry room. At times, I was a nurse when my mom went through two big injuries that left her temporarily immobilized. Whatever was needed at the time, that's what I did, and that's where I found my purpose.

It was through this part of my journey that I learned the very important truth that God created each of us for the purpose of service. We are called first to serve Him, and then out of that calling, we are called to serve others.

We are called first to serve God, and then out of that calling, we are called to serve. others.

Jesus set the example for this when He came to earth and took on the role of One Who did not come to be served, but to serve, and to give His life as a ransom for many. (Matthew 20:28)

I love the way it is described in Philippians 2:3-8,

> **Don't push your way to the front; don't sweet-talk your way to the top. Put yourself aside, and**

> **help others get ahead.**
>
> **Don't be obsessed with getting your own advantage. Forget yourselves long enough to lend a helping hand.**
>
> **Think of yourselves the way Christ Jesus thought of himself.**
>
> **He had equal status with God but didn't think so much of himself that he had to cling to the advantages of that status no matter what. Not at all.**
>
> **When the time came, he set aside the privileges of deity and took on the status of a slave, became human!**
>
> **Having become human, he stayed human. It was an incredibly humbling process.**
>
> **He didn't claim special privileges. Instead, he lived a selfless, obedient life and then died a selfless, obedient death—and the worst kind of death at that—a crucifixion. (The Message).**

What a powerful scripture! Honestly, I love the way the Message says it so plainly and challenges us to think beyond society's normal think-of-yourself-advance-yourself agenda.

Instead, we are told to lay these things aside as followers of Christ and think and act as He did. Rather than seeking to advance ourselves, we are called to be a servant as Jesus was a servant. To do that, I think we need to take a few minutes and really look at the ways that Jesus was a servant.

First, as Philippians says, He chose to come to earth as a man. Even though He was fully God with all of the characteristics and power of Deity, He willingly laid that aside and took on a human body with all of its frailties and limitations. Leaving behind the riches and opulence of Heaven, He allowed Himself to be born among poor working people in a small town. From this perspective, He experienced real life with all of its struggles. He dealt with family, friends, financial issues, and all of the things we deal with in our everyday lives. He did it for us—-so that He could identify with our weaknesses and lift us up before the Heavenly Father. (Hebrews 4:15-16)

As He grew, we see Jesus taking on the form of a servant when He submits to His earthly parents, Mary and Joseph, and returns with them from Jerusalem. (Luke 2:51)

Then in His silent years until He turned thirty, He worked in a carpenter's shop doing manual labor, providing for His widowed mother and His brothers and sisters.

At the beginning of His ministry, He demonstrates humility by submitting to baptism by John the Baptist. Think about it, as the Messiah, Jesus could have approached John with the attitude of *"I'm here now. You're out, I'm in."* Instead, He went to John and demonstrated humility by asking to be baptized. (Matthew 3:13-17)

Throughout the next three years, we see Him demonstrating servanthood in His ministry as He was constantly freely giving to people. Rather than coming onto the scene as a ruler who demanded respect and setting up a kingdom, He spent His days and His energy healing sick people, casting out demons, teaching everyone who would listen (not just the religious or the elite), and discipling twelve men about the kingdom of God.

Then came what would perhaps be one of His greatest lessons to His disciples, the night He washed their feet and then served them communion. I find it so valuable that in His last moments, during the Last Supper, Jesus took the time to teach them, once again, the value of servanthood.

Within minutes they were bickering over who of them would end up the greatest.

> **But Jesus intervened: "Kings like to throw their weight around and people in authority like to give themselves fancy titles. It's not going to be that way with you. Let the senior among you become like the junior; let the leader act the part of the servant.**
>
> **Who would you rather be: the one who eats the dinner or the one who serves the dinner? You'd rather eat and be served, right? But I've taken my place among you as the one who serves."**
>
> **(Luke 22:24-27).**

After this, He made His greatest demonstration of being a servant, when He submitted to God's will and was crucified for the sins of all of mankind. Even though He was sinless, like a servant, He took the punishment that we deserved so that we could experience a restored relationship with God.

Following His example, Philippians 2 makes it clear that it is God's will for all of His children to imitate Christ's attitude and put on servanthood.

How do we do this?

It starts by understanding that we were created to be servants. This is our purpose.

Our place is serving God and serving others.

Whatever the opportunity to serve, we should do it with passion.

Now I know, the last one is hard to imagine. I mean, how can you be passionate about cleaning the bathroom?

Here's what I've learned:

Even if you're not passionate about what you're doing, you can be passionate about Who you are doing it for.

In my own life, I've developed this attitude. I found purpose in my daily chores and routines because I knew that God had called me to that place and His purpose for me was to serve my family in that season. Rather than looking at my jobs as a burden, I saw them as a calling and said, *"If this is how You want me to serve You, then I will do the best job that I can."*

Even if you're not passionate about what you're doing, you can be passionate about Who you are doing it for.

Over the years, I've come to believe that this is a key to finding your passion, your place, and your purpose in life:

> **"Whatever you do, work at it with all your heart, as working for the Lord, not for human masters, since you know that you will receive an inheritance from the Lord as a reward. It is the Lord Christ you are serving." (Colossians 3:23-24)**

You see, the key to finding purpose and passion in every place that God puts you is realizing that you aren't just doing a job, you are fulfilling a calling. Whatever responsibility God has placed in your life, God has given it to you for a purpose.

Everything that you do is your calling, and as a Christian,

you are working for God.

When you truly adopt this attitude in your life, everything changes—-especially you. When you embrace this truth, you are no longer just putting in time or getting through a list of things to do. Instead, you come to the realization that whatever you are doing is part of God's purpose. It's not just a job; it's a calling, and God has a plan to use you, right where you are, to influence your world for Him.

This is how you find purpose even in jobs that seem menial. It's how you become passionate about the mundane: when you realize that everything you do—-even the dirtiest, most unappreciated jobs—when done for Jesus, help fulfill His kingdom purpose.

When I discovered this truth, my whole attitude toward my life changed!

Now I wasn't just cleaning toilets and doing laundry because I loved my family (which was a valuable reason in itself). Instead, I was cleaning toilets and doing laundry for Jesus. If I was doing it for Him, then I was going to do the best job I possibly could! Somehow as I continued in this mindset, I genuinely came to the place where I no longer worried about advancing myself or finding a way out of my life, but I really began to enjoy it.

When I adopted this attitude, I found my purpose was to serve Jesus in everything I do. I found my place: serving Jesus by serving my family. I found my passion: serving Jesus by serving others.

You see the problem with selfish ambition and vain conceit is that they keep our eyes always focused on ourselves. What can I do for me? How can I make my life better? How can I advance my agenda and my cause?

However, when we adopt follow Jesus' example and take on the attitude of a servant, we find that the world is so much bigger than our selfish view. God's plan is so much greater than just making us happy and comfortable. Instead, God's plan is eternal. His focus is seeing men and women come into a relationship with Him. His purpose for you and me isn't to advance ourselves, but rather, to come into agreement with Him and do whatever job He gives us so that His agenda can be carried out.

Most of the time, this doesn't involve being served. Instead, it involves working hard, getting our hands dirty, and saying, *"God, whatever role You want me to fill, I'm there ready and willing to serve."*

It's when we adopt this attitude that we are truly on the road to finding our purpose in life.

At least that's how it worked for me.

When I stopped worrying about how to make Adessa great and started focusing on making Jesus great in everything I did, my life truly began to change. Then rather than seeing my responsibilities as a chore, I found joy and fulfillment in them. I began seeing that no job was beneath me and that it really was a pleasure to serve in any available capacity.

As time went on and life began to transition and change, I continued to carry this attitude with me. You see, there came a point in my life when my role of taking care of my family ended when my mom suddenly passed away. During this time, among all of the intense grief and pain, I once again had to ask *"What now God? What do You want to do with my life?"*

One of the biggest differences between the girl who asked this question after college and the woman who asked fifteen years later was her attitude toward servanthood. Over the years of being at home, I learned that any opportunity to serve Jesus truly is a privilege. I don't need the limelight. I just want to do what I can for Him.

This is an attitude that my brother and I work very hard at adopting into every area of 4One Ministries. At home and on the job we have a motto: *"It doesn't matter whose job it is. If it needs done, do it."*

If this means stuffing envelopes to send out conferences advertisements, then we do it with joy for Jesus. If it means carrying boxes or setting up tables, then it's our privilege because we are doing it to advance a kingdom cause. Whether I'm working on Men's Ministry or Women's Ministry, it really doesn't matter. I'm serving Jesus, and it's my privilege to be able to minister to women but also work behind the scenes to see that Men's Ministry is advanced.

We adopted the same attitude while volunteering at our local church: whatever you want us to do, we will be there. It's why Jamie ran the sound system, why we volunteered to cook meals for an inner city Christmas party, and why we loved working in children's ministry. Over the years we learned that every opportunity to serve Jesus is a privilege. We don't need a title; it's just an honor to serve.

From my personal experience, I honestly believe that this is a truth that anyone who is seeking their purpose in life needs to learn.

As followers of Jesus, we are called to serve. This is our purpose.

While I don't know exactly how God wants you to serve Him and the people around you, I do know the attitude He wants you to have in every area of your life.

He wants you to imitate Jesus and think of others before

yourself.

He wants you to see each area of your life and each responsibility you are given as an opportunity to work for God and bring Him glory. This applies to your family life, your work life, and every area of your personal life.

The truth is the world has more than enough people who are looking to advance themselves and their agenda. What the kingdom of God really needs is servants.

People who are willing to do anything that God asks them to do just because they love Jesus and want to see His kingdom advanced.

I truly believe that when you allow the Holy Spirit to develop this attitude inside of you, your life will find meaning. When Jesus is your passion, and you realize that your place is serving Him, He will lead you to your purpose.

Study Questions:

1. Read Philippians 2:3-8. What description of servanthood stands out most to you?

2. How did Jesus take on the form of a servant?

3. The chapter says, *"Even if you're not passionate about what you're doing, you can be passionate about Who you are doing it for."* How can you apply this in your life?

4. Read Colossians 3:23-24. How can you apply this Scripture in your life?

5. What is the key to finding passion and purpose in every place that God places you?

6. After reading this chapter, are there areas of your life where you need to adjust your attitude toward servanthood?

7. What are some practical steps that you can take to follow Jesus' example of servanthood?

8. How will adopting the attitude of a servant help you find your passion, your place and your purpose?

Chapter 11

LIVING A LIFE WORTHY OF YOUR CALLING

It was a day or two after my mom went to Heaven. Jamie and I were alone in the living room waiting for our friends and relatives to arrive at the house, when Jamie picked up my mom's Bible. Randomly, he opened it and began reading Philippians 2:12-16. It had always been one of my mom's favorite verses. That day it seemed to jump off the page at us.

> **Therefore, my dear friends, as you have always obeyed—not only in my presence, but now much more in my absence—continue to work out your salvation with fear and trembling, for it is God who works in you to will and to act in order to fulfill his good purpose.**
>
> **Do everything without grumbling or arguing,**

> **so that you may become blameless and pure, 'children of God without fault in a warped and crooked generation.'**
>
> **Then you will shine among them like stars in the sky as you hold firmly to the word of life. And then I will be able to boast on the day of Christ that I did not run or labor in vain. (New International Version).**

At a moment in time when Jamie and I were completely lost in grief, these words spoke purpose to us, reminding us who we were and how we were called to live. It reminded us of lessons that our mom taught us while we were growing up and throughout our lives. Namely, that as Christians we are called to live pure lives in an impure world. We are called to be set apart, to live differently, and to be so grateful for our salvation that we accept our purpose of living blameless lives that honor Jesus.

This was one of my mom's passions. Now that she was gone, it was as if she was passing the mantle of this passion onto us.

Over the many years since she went to Heaven, I've thought about this Scripture.

In fact, when practical matters made it necessary for Jamie and I to combine our two ministries into one non-profit corporation, we thought about this Scripture as we were trying to come up with a name. Ultimately, it was pondering on this Scripture that led us to a similar Scripture, Ephesians 4:1, which inspired not only the name for our ministry (4One Ministries) but helped us define our purpose. To us, it seemed like a shorter version of Philippians 2:12-16. Again, Paul is imparting purpose to a young church with his words: **"As a prisoner for the Lord, then, I urge you to live a life worthy**

of the calling you have received." (Ephesians 4:1).

This is a line that you will see repeated over and over again as you read through the New Testament. *"Live a life worthy of the calling you have received."*

What does it mean?

Basically, it means, *"living up to the family name."* 1 John 5:1-3 explains it this way:

> **Every person who believes that Jesus is, in fact, the Messiah, is God-begotten.**
>
> **If we love the One who conceives the child, we'll surely love the child who was conceived.**
>
> **The reality test on whether or not we love God's children is this: Do we love God? Do we keep his commands?**
>
> **The proof that we love God comes when we keep his commandments and they are not at all troublesome. (The Message).**

I like to think of it this way: Have you ever seen the movie, *The Princess Diaries?*[1]

If you haven't, you should (but not now because you need to finish this chapter).

In the meantime, I'll tell you about it.

The Princess Diaries focuses on the life of Mia Thermopolis, a teenage girl living with her mother in San Francisco. When we first meet Mia, she's a bit shy, very afraid, and well, a bit on the unpopular side. Perhaps she describes herself best when she says that "*her goal in life is to be invisible.*"

Unfortunately for Mia, this aspiration is blown to smithereens when her grandmother, Queen Clarisse Renaldi, arrives with the news that Mia is a princess. Due to an unforeseen turn of events, Mia can no longer wait until she is an adult to assume her title and responsibilities (as was the original plan). She needed to begin stepping into her calling immediately.

As you can imagine, this was quite a shock for a young girl. One day she was just an average, ordinary teenager trying to pass gym class, and the next she is expected to rule a country!

Oh, and there's one more thing—-before she can actually step into her role, Mia has to take *"princess lessons."* She needs to learn how to think, act, speak, and present herself as a royal. After all, she is being given a great responsibility. Before she can be who she was born to be, she needed to learn how to *"live a life worthy of her calling."*

The same is true for us.

When you and I accept God's offer of salvation, it wasn't just a "*get-into-Heaven-free card.*" It was so much more. As it says in John 1:12, we were literally adopted into the family of God.

What an amazing privilege!

Yet as 1 John 5:1-3 explains, with this awesome privilege comes responsibility.

Just like Mia couldn't accept the title of *"princess"* and continue living however she chose, when we become a part of God's family, we need to begin learning to live as children of God.

Why is this so important?

This question is answered in our original verse, Philippians 2:13: **"For it is God who works in you to will and to act in order to fulfill his good purpose." (New International Version).**

Here is a beautiful truth: God has a plan and a purpose for your life. From the day you were born, God had a design for your life that only you can fulfill. There are people He wants you to help, lives He wants you to reach, and a purpose that He wants you to complete. From the day of your conception, He has been looking forward to the day when you will fulfill that plan.

It is absolutely necessary that we submit to living a life worthy of our calling before we can step into all that God has for us.

When you gave your life to Jesus and accepted His offer of salvation, that was the first step on the path to fulfilling His purpose for your life. But it was only the beginning. The next steps are allowing Him, day by day, to make you into a new creation, to teach you how to live by His Word and according to His kingdom rules, and to mold you and shape you into the image of His Son, Jesus Christ.

If you will allow Him to take you through this process, then He will prepare you to step into the complete plan and purpose that He has for your life. However, just like Mia had to submit to *"princess lessons"* before she could become a queen, it is absolutely necessary that we submit to living a life worthy of our calling before we can step into all that God has for us.

It really is our choice.

Sadly, it's a choice that far too many people reject.

Instead, they come to Jesus but they don't want to learn God's ways and submit to God's laws. They want to carry the family name and reap the benefits of being part of the family, but they are unwilling to live a life worthy of their calling.

Sadly, because they are unwilling to let the Holy Spirit work in their hearts, forsake their sin and develop the character traits that God wants to develop in their lives, God is unable to give them the responsibilities that would accompany fully stepping into their purpose and calling. It's not that God takes away His calling or purpose. Instead, these people abdicate their purpose and calling because they are unwilling to accept the responsibility.

To me, this is one of the saddest stories ever....when God offers someone the world and they say, *"No thanks, I'd rather stay the way I am."* Yet, I've seen it over and over again.

Thankfully, this is not the way it has to be. Instead, each one of us can make the choice that Mia made and submit to the Holy Spirit's work of making us into the people we need to be to fulfill God's purpose in our lives.

How do we do this?

2 **Timothy 3:15-17 says, "There's nothing like the written Word of God for showing you the way to salvation through faith in Christ Jesus. Every part of Scripture is God-breathed and useful one way or another—showing us truth, exposing our rebellion, correcting our mistakes, training us to live God's way. Through the Word we are put together and shaped up for the tasks God has for us."**
(The Message).

The first step in living a life worthy of your calling is making the choice to read God's Word and learn what is says. In a world where everything is acceptable and truth is relative, our chief tool in learning God's ways is knowing His Word. The Bible clearly defines what God considers righteous living and what God considers sinful living.

I love the way the Message states the last part of this verse: **"Through the Word we are put together and shaped up for the tasks God has for us."**

It's right there! It is only through God's Word that the Holy Spirit can shape us to fulfill the plans and purposes that God has for our lives. If we are going to live pure and blameless lives before God, we need to find out what the Bible says and apply it to our daily lives.

That last sentence contains a key element: *We don't just need to hear God's Word, we need to apply it to our daily lives.* We need to make it practical and hear what God's Word has to say about each and every situation we encounter.

This is where things start to get personal and extremely practical.

Let's start by reading what Paul said when he was being very personal and practical with the church in Thessalonica as he encouraged them to live a life worthy of their calling.

> **Finally, dear brothers and sisters, we urge you in the name of the Lord Jesus to live in a way that pleases God, as we have taught you.....**
>
> **....For you remember what we taught you by the authority of the Lord Jesus. God's will is for you to be holy, so stay away from all sexual sin.**
>
> **Then each of you will control his own body and live in holiness and honor— not in lustful passion like the pagans who do not know God and his ways...**

....God has called us to live holy lives, not impure lives.

Therefore, anyone who refuses to live by these rules is not disobeying human teaching but is rejecting God, who gives his Holy Spirit to you. (New Living Translation, 1 Thessalonians 4:1-8).

Living a life worthy of our calling means living holy and pure lives.

Just because an activity is socially acceptable, even among church people, doesn't mean that it is Biblically acceptable.

Sadly, this is not normal in our culture. We live in a world where even the grossest sin is considered acceptable and lesser sins are considered normal and healthy. Much like Paul described the world of his day, our society is a *"warped and crooked generation."*

Which gives us the same calling as the church in Paul's day to *"Shine among them like stars in the sky as you hold firmly to the Word of life."*

Here are some practical ways that we can fulfill this part of our purpose:

Choosing Purity in Our Activities

Part of making a choice to "*live a life worthy of our calling*" will involve allowing the Bible to determine whether or not we will participate in an activity.

Here's an important truth: Just because an activity is socially acceptable, even among church people, doesn't mean that it is Biblically acceptable.

For example, my friend told me about a wedding shower to which she wasn't invited because the people hosting the party were planning some inappropriate activities and games that they knew my friend would find objectionable. Oddly enough, the party was being held in her church! (She's married to the pastor.) Rather than allowing her commitment to Biblical standards to convict them of their sin, they chose to leave her name off of the list. Even if she would have been invited, she wouldn't have participated because she is dedicated to living a life worthy of her calling.

Compare this to the woman who talks about how much she loves Jesus but posts pics on social media of a bridal shower filled with inappropriate party favors of a very *"adult"* nature. Or the Christian who goes to the strip club because it's her close friend's bachelorette party and she can't hurt her feelings. Or the single girl who spent a Friday night watching an "R" rated movie about male strippers with her girlfriends and then took her place on the worship team on Sunday morning.

Just in case no one has told you before: These things are not okay. They are sin.

According to the Bible we are to **"Come out from them and be separate." (2 Corinthians 6:17).**

We aren't supposed to blend in but be a light in the dark world. (Matthew 5:16)

There shouldn't even be the hint of the world's sexual sin found among us. (Ephesians 5:3)

Even though I know this is hard for some people to hear, sometimes hard truths are the most loving thing we can share. So here it is:

As children of God, we cannot do whatever we want, go

wherever we want, and participate in any sin that we choose and still experience the blessing of God on our lives. Each of us needs to come to the point where we decide whether we want to enjoy the temporary pleasure of sin or live a blameless and pure life so that we can enjoy God's complete plan and purpose for our lives.

Of course, choosing purity and holiness goes beyond choosing our activities. We also need to practice:

Choosing Purity in Our Speech

This is another area where our changing culture has affected our behavior.

Years ago, women were taught to speak in a ladylike fashion. Women were discouraged from using vulgarity or speaking crudely.

In more modern times, it's become a badge of honor for women to speak in an unseemly manner. In all forms of entertainment, women are seen laughing and telling dirty jokes, swearing, and speaking in a very vulgar manner. However, these things are unacceptable for the Christian woman.

> **Ephesians 5:3-8 says: "But among you there must not be even a hint of sexual immorality, or of any kind of impurity, or of greed, because these are improper for God's holy people. Nor should there be obscenity, foolish talk or coarse joking, which are out of place, but rather thanksgiving."**

If we are going to be daughters of the King who live by Kingdom principles, we need to conform our speech to these standards. I know that this can be difficult at times, mainly because this type of sinful behavior has become acceptable in the church. Unfortunately, many have adopted the attitude that it's okay to tell an off-color joke or speak in a vulgar manner—especially if you're not in mixed company. I've been in this situation many times when a group of Christian women were sitting around talking like sailors on shore-leave.

For instance, how many of us have been with a group of Christian women when someone in the group decides to talk openly about their sexual experiences? Have you ever been with someone who saw a movie or television show that you knew was too racy, yet you allowed them to tell you about it?

I was in Bible college the first time I experienced this type of female conversation. Honestly, I was shocked! One by one, women who had experiences were sharing every detail of their past encounters with anyone who would listen. With vivid images, they were bragging about their sexual history before they became Christians.

It wasn't long until I realized that this was a common practice among Christian women. However, it doesn't matter how common or accepted this type of conversation seems, according to Biblical standards it is wrong. In the first place, those who are telling the story are bragging about sins they are supposed to be sorry they committed. Reliving the experience over and over again through the art of storytelling isn't a sign of repentance or regret. Rather, it is a signal that they need to continue working on the areas of their mind and soul that still deal with impure thoughts.

On the other hand, those who choose to listen to the stories are just as guilty.

Honestly, what is the difference between listening to someone tell of their sexual encounters and watching a couple have sex on television? In both cases, you are filling your mind with sexual images and ignoring Paul's command to live a pure and blameless life.

I understand that it's difficult to be the one who says, *"I can't participate in this type of conversation because it's sin."* However, this is exactly what Christian women need to do. We need to stand up for what is right and stop participating in impure conversations.

The truth is that how we speak defines our identity. If we want to be recognized as Christian women and daughters of God, our speech needs to reflect His image.

Our conversation should fit the description in Colossians 4:6: ***"Let your conversation be always full of grace, seasoned with salt, so that you may know how to answer everyone."***

Choosing Purity in Our Entertainment

As Christian woman, we need to be aware of how easy it is to be influenced by society's view of women. They say we need to be sexy, we need to be open to many sexual experiences, and they mock those who choose to hold to Biblical purity. Let's honestly ask ourselves, *"What are the mediums that send us these messages?"*

The answer is easy. It is television, movies, music, books, magazines, videos, and advertising. These mediums are especially dangerous for women because as we get into the storyline, we tend to become emotionally involved. We laugh at the heroine's blunders, and we cry as they endure their struggles. We watch the romance grow between characters and wait for them to finally realize they are in love. Then because we want to see the end of the story, we ignore the fact that their romance ends in the bedroom instead of at the wedding altar. Slowly we become desensitized and begin rationalizing and compromising with sin. Even though we have not sinned ourselves, we have just watched other people sin in the name of entertainment. Ladies, this is not living by

Biblical standards.

The Bible says in Philippians 4:8: **"Finally, brothers and sisters, whatever is true, whatever is noble, whatever is right, whatever is pure, whatever is lovely, whatever is admirable—if anything is excellent or praiseworthy—think about such things."**

Notice this Scripture speaks to brothers and sisters. Too often, we believe the lie that only men struggle with these issues. What a lie! As Christian women, we need to apply this standard to our lives as well.

The same thing applies to reading material. You can't fill your mind with magazine articles and romance novels containing sexually explicit content and expect to keep your mind pure. Sometimes even Christian novelists cross the line and tell stories that are too sexually graphic. Don't read these books. Instead, read books that encourage you in your endeavor toward purity and fill your mind with good thoughts.

At our house, we have established certain guidelines for our entertainment choices, specifically our television viewing, that we feel help us maintain a pure lifestyle. First, we set the parental controls on our television to PG with sexual content blocked. This helps eliminate programs with a sexually explicit nature.

Secondly, we avoid all sex scenes. Years ago, my favorite pastor's wife taught us that whenever you watch a couple in bed together, you are watching pornography. Her teaching has become a rule at our house. Whenever a program turns toward a bedroom scene, we turn it off. We do not need those images replaying in our minds.

We've also installed the Covenant Eyes program (an

internet accountability and filtering system) that blocks content on our computers and phones for online accountability.

As you stop filling your mind with these images and messages, you will stop being influenced by the world's thinking. Your conscience will stop being desensitized to accept sin, and you will start becoming sensitive to the conviction of the Holy Spirit. Most importantly, you will stop measuring your image of yourself by the standards of the world. This will help you to conform to God's standard of purity for His daughters.

Choosing to Present Ourselves in a Godly Manner

One of the biggest way that society has infiltrated the minds of women is with the lie that we need to be *"sexy."* We need to look sexy. We need to dress sexy. Our hairstyle needs to be sexy. Our shoes need to be sexy. We need to wear pants that make our backside look sexy. Tops need to be as revealing and sexy as possible. Advertisements tell us that we even need to smell sexy.

Personally, I find it very ironic that in a society that claims to be *"liberal"* and *"feminist,"* it is the Bible that actually has more respect for women. In God's kingdom, a woman's value isn't determined by her appearance or her sex appeal. Rather, a woman is valuable because she is a human being who God loves. Because God loves you, He wants you to excel in every area of your life—physically, mentally, emotionally and spiritually. He appreciates your skills, talents, and abilities. He is constantly working in your life to make

> I find it very ironic that in a society that claims to be "liberal" and "feminist," it is the Bible that actually has more respect for women.

you the strongest, most capable woman that you can be.

Now before anyone freaks out, let me say that I am not going to give you a lecture on what not to wear, nor will I to say that Christian women should not dress in the most attractive manner possible. I will not give a list of *"do's"* and *"don'ts"* or make a judgment about your choices.

Honestly, I don't think I need to do this. I believe that inside of every woman we know the difference between an outfit that makes us feel beautiful and self-confident and an outfit that makes us feel sexy. As Christian women, we need to make the conscious choice to choose to wear things that make us feel good about ourselves and avoid wearing things that actually degrade us.

As we're shopping, we need to ask ourselves, *"Does this outfit tell the world that I am a strong, confident, Christian woman? Am I presenting myself to the world as a woman with high standards of purity? Is there anyone or anywhere that would make me feel uncomfortable or immodest wearing this outfit?"*

That's why this point is entitled *"presenting ourselves in a pure manner."* Honestly, it isn't about a certain type of clothing you should or shouldn't wear—it's about how you present yourself to the world. What does your appearance say about you?

Does your outfit say, *"I am a woman who is living a life worthy of her calling?"*

Ultimately, that is the question we need to be asking ourselves about every area of our lives.

"Am I living up to my potential as a King's daughter?"

"Am I obeying the rules of the kingdom in every area of my life?"

"Is my life a positive reflection of my Heavenly Father, the King of the Universe?"“

"How should a Christian woman conduct herself in today's world?"

As you answer these questions remember that God isn't giving you these guidelines to restrict you. Rather, He is developing you. He is preparing you. Just like Queen Clarisse mentored Mia so that she could step into the destiny she was born to fulfill, so is God's Word making you into the woman who will fulfill God's plan and purpose for your life. That's why living a life worthy of your calling should be your passion.

Study Questions:

1. What does *"living a life worthy of your calling"* have to do with finding your passion, place, and purpose in life?
2. Read John 1:12. What does it mean to you to be adopted into God's family? What benefits does this adoption bring?
3. What does it mean to *"abdicate"* God's purpose for your life? How can you avoid making this choice?
4. This chapter says, *"Just because an activity is socially acceptable, even among church people, doesn't mean that it is Biblically acceptable."* What does this quote mean to you?
5. Read 2 Corinthians 6:17, Matthew 5:16, and Ephesians 5:3. What do these verses tell us about living a life worthy of our calling?
6. This chapter frequently references Philippians 4:8. How can we practically use the principles taught in this verse to *"live a life worthy of our calling?"*
7. What principle stood out most to you in this chapter?

Chapter 12

SALT AND LIGHT

"Therefore go and make disciples of all nations, baptizing them in the name of the Father and of the Son and of the Holy Spirit, and teaching them to obey everything I have commanded you. And surely I am with you always, to the very end of the age." Matthew 28:19-20 (NIV)

Just before He ascended to Heaven, these were the last words Jesus spoke to His disciples—the mission and purpose for all Christians throughout time. Unlike Ethan Hunt, who is given his mission and asked if he would accept it, the Great Commission is not an option, it is a command. It's a directive from Jesus to His followers regarding how they are to live every part of their lives.

And yet, if I'm being completely honest, when I was younger, I'd read this Scripture or hear a sermon on this verse and immediately panic thinking, *"But I don't feel a call to foreign missions."* I'd wonder if there was something wrong with me that I had no desire to travel the world or minister overseas. Was I not committed to Jesus? Why didn't I have the same vision as my friends who do such admirable work around the world?

Was my calling less significant or important? Is it possible to live the Great Commission when God hasn't called you into foreign missions?

Of course, as I grew older I realized that we all have unique callings and most of us are not called overseas. Instead, we are called to be salt and light in the places we live to the people in our lives. As it says in Matthew 5:13-16,

> **Let me tell you why you are here. You're here to be salt-seasoning that brings out the God-flavors of this earth. If you lose your saltiness, how will people taste godliness? You've lost your usefulness and will end up in the garbage.**
>
> **Here's another way to put it: You're here to be light, bringing out the God- colors in the world.**
>
> **God is not a secret to be kept. We're going public with this, as public as a city on a hill.**
>
> **If I make you light-bearers, you don't think I'm going to hide you under a bucket, do you? I'm putting you on a light stand.**
>
> **Now that I've put you there on a hilltop, on a light stand—shine! Keep open house; be generous with your lives.**
>
> **By opening up to others, you'll prompt people to open up with God, this generous Father in heaven. (The Message).**

In this passage, Jesus describes how most of us will find our purpose and fulfill our part of the Great Commission: by sharing the love of Jesus with our families, our friends, in our communities, our workplaces, and with all the people we come in contact with during the course of our lives.

The problem arises when we develop the attitude that because we're not called to go to a far away, exotic mission field, we lose our passion for the Great Commission. Sadly, this loss of passion results in us ignoring our God-Given purpose to fulfill the Great Commission in our little corner of the world.

The truth is that even if you're not called to be Billy Graham, you are called to share the Gospel with your neighbors, the girl who bags your groceries, and the woman who sits across from you at work.

You don't have to be a nationally known speaker to lead a Bible study in your home or teach a class of young girls.

You don't have to wait for Bethel Music to call with a contract before you can volunteer to sing background vocals on Wednesday night.

Then there's perhaps the most important truth: that 95% of fulfilling the Great Commission involves absolutely no limelight at all. In fact, it is carried out by those who are willing to love, listen, and share their testimony of what God has done in their lives. For most of us, this is the version of the Great Commission that we are called to fulfill. Until we accept this challenge, we will continue to lack the fulfillment and joy that comes with fulfilling this purpose in our lives.

95% of fulfilling the Great Commission involves absolutely no limelight at all.

So how do we begin fulfilling our purpose in the Great Commission?

It starts by being salt and light—-by being an example to the world around you.

We live in a world that desperately needs a taste of godliness. Just as salt changes the flavor whenever it is added to a dish, so we are called to change the flavor of the world around us. In an environment of hopelessness, anger, hatred, and fear, we are called to provide a taste of hope, love, and the kind of peace that comes from a living relationship with God. Most often this isn't spoken by our words, but rather, through the way we live our lives.

Years ago my favorite pastor expressed it this way:

"Present Jesus to the world like a shiny red apple—-so appealing that they just can't wait to take a bite."

Although I might've used the example of chocolate cake (because I love chocolate cake), the sentiment is the same: we need to make Jesus look good to the world around us.

Does this mean that we just walk around with our head in the clouds acting like obnoxious super-spiritual robots?

Absolutely not! The truth is that the world isn't looking for any more phonies. What people are looking for is kindness. Friendliness. Genuine concern for other people.

Many years ago, the Holy Spirit began impressing on my heart the need to demonstrate God's love to the people I come in contact with using these traits. To practice showing love, I began forcing myself to be kind to the cashier at the grocery store, the bank teller, or department stores cashiers. Even if the line was long and other people were being rude and complaining, I'd choose to be friendly, to make conversation, and to try to encourage.

I have to admit, the response was pretty amazing! People were actually surprised! They were so used to being ignored or treated badly that it changed their day when someone chose to be kind. Over time going to the same businesses, we actually started to be friends with the employees. One woman at the gas station actually comes to our car every time we see her just to chat. Over time, I've been able to share with her about our lives and Jesus. Yet it all started with a smile and a friendly, *"Beautiful day, isn't it?"*

In a world that is so desperate for simple kindness, this story can be repeated over and over again. As we simply make the choice to treat people with kindness and respect, to show interest in their lives, and to listen to their stories, we are sprinkling God's love into their lives and making them wonder, *"Why are they so different?"*

When they see us having hope through our struggles, expressing joy even though our darkest days, and choosing to do the right thing even when it's obvious there is an easier way, people begin to wonder, *"Why? Why do you care? Why are you concerned? Why are you different?"* That opens the door for us to fulfill our purpose: to share the Gospel of Jesus with them.

Another way to add the flavor of godliness into the world is through demonstrating love and generosity in difficult situations. For instance, years ago one of my neighbor's children was in a horrible accident. Every day they were driving back and forth to the hospital, and every night for weeks, Mom and I made them dinner so they would come home to a hot meal. To us, it wasn't a big deal, we just made a little extra; to them, it showed concern. It gave us the opportunity to show them the love of Jesus.

We did the same thing from time to time for my parent's friend who was going through cancer treatments. This lady loved to talk! Whenever we would drop off the food, we'd allow plenty of time to let her talk about whatever she wanted. In our conversations, we'd share about Jesus in the hopes that she'd make a commitment to Him. What a tremendous blessing it was when her daughter told us that before she died, she prayed with the 700 Club to become a Christian.

This is just a minuscule example of how choosing to go a little out of your way to help someone else can change the flavor of a situation. Even if it doesn't lead to a conversion, every time you choose to insert God's love into a situation, you are planting a seed that the Holy Spirit can use to continue to draw someone to Him. You don't know what He can do with your kindness, your conversation, or your acts of generosity to draw someone to Jesus over time.

That's why it's important that in our quest for purpose, we allow the Holy Spirit to show us each and every opportunity to demonstrate life with Jesus in an appealing way to those around us. As we do this among our families, in our communities, at our jobs, and in our social situations we are doing our part to fulfill the Great Commission. We're filling our place and sharing our passion for Jesus with the world. Worst case scenario, we've planted a seed. Best case scenario we are given the opportunity to answer the question, *"What makes you live the way you do?"*

This leads us to the next way we can fulfill the Great Commission: ***by sharing our testimony.***

Over the years, I've come to the conclusion that the greatest tool that we have to change the world is through our personal testimony. There is nothing more powerful than the testimony of a life that was changed and revolutionized by

Jesus Christ.

We see this exhibited in one of my favorite stories in the Bible: the story of the woman at the well in John 4.

When we first meet this woman, her life is a mess. She's lived a sinful life and everybody knows it. Because of her past, she has become an outcast from society and is basically trying to avoid everybody. Then she has an encounter with Jesus that changes her life.

If you read through the chapter, you'll see that Jesus talked her through abandoning religion and moving into a personal relationship with Him.

Then He gave her a choice, "Do you want what I have to offer?" Her decision changed her life. That's when we see the most amazing thing happen.

> **The woman left her water jar beside the well and ran back to the village, telling everyone, "Come and see a man who told me everything I ever did! Could he possibly be the Messiah?"**
>
> **So the people came streaming from the village to see him. (John 4:28-30, NLT).**

Here's the best part:

> **Many Samaritans from the village believed in Jesus because the woman had said, "He told me everything I ever did!" (John 4:39, NLT).**

It was this woman's testimony that changed her town. Because she was willing to share her testimony, including acknowledging her past, many of the Samaritans in her town believed in Jesus. Yet none of these people would have come to Jesus, had it not been for the woman at the well's willingness to come out of hiding and share her testimony with other people.

From her testimony sprang a community of people who believed that Jesus was the Messiah. In a few years, this community was probably the basis of the church in Samaria. It all began with one woman who was desperate for a change and received that change from Jesus.

Today, the question that each of us has to answer is: ***Will we follow her example?***

God has bigger plans for your life than just making you comfortable. He wants you to play a role in influencing and changing the world around you.

Because the truth is that God didn't just save you, adopt you into His family, and make you into a new creation exclusively for your own benefit. Yes, He did it because He loves you and wants what is the absolute best for you, but He's also working in your life and making you into a new creation because He deeply and passionately loves the people in the world around you. He wants to use YOU to introduce them to a personal, life-changing relationship with Him.

God has bigger plans for your life than just making you comfortable. He wants you to play a role in influencing and changing the world around you. He wants to use you to touch hurting hearts, to bring people to Him, to help mend families and restore broken lives. He wants you to learn His Word so that after it has revolutionized your life, you can then teach His Word to others saying, *"This is how God changed my life. I used to struggle with all of these sins and heartaches, but these principles in God's Word set me free. Because I obeyed the Bible I have joy, peace, courage, strength, and hope in my life."*

Sometimes when we hear this truth, our first response can be, *"But I don't want everyone to know my story. There are parts of it that are shameful and embarrassing. Why do people need to know my personal business?"*

Being completely vulnerable, I'll admit that this was a struggle for me. When God began changing our lives and opening doors for ministry, it was very tempting to simply thank God for all that He did and enjoy the benefits. I was pretty sure that I didn't want people to know about my failures or the issues that the Holy Spirit helped me overcome. Did I really want people to know about all my problems? Even more difficult was sharing the story of all that my family had gone through. I wondered if it was wrong to share family secrets, and I didn't want to relive the pain of the many events that I preferred to keep behind me.

Trust me when I say that it was ridiculously tempting to just keep it quiet, continue with our *"perfect"* image and thank God for the benefits we were enjoying. But the Holy Spirit made it very clear to us that it would be wrong for us to do that.

You see, with privilege comes responsibility. When you and I experience the privilege of experiencing God's forgiveness, salvation, healing, and restoration, we have a responsibility to share our testimony with others. The truth is that your testimony doesn't belong to you---it belongs to God. It is the story of His grace, His mercy, His compassion, and His miraculous power.

As a recipient of all of those things, you and I have a responsibility to shout it from the rooftops. We can let the whole world see, through our lives, that there is a God Who saves, delivers, and heals, and He wants to change ALL lives.

That is why I share my testimony. It's why I speak and write books and completely open myself up---because I am so grateful for what God has done in my life that I can't help but share it with others.

But this doesn't just apply to me. It applies to every single person who has been saved by grace. The question each of us needs to answer is: *"Do you care enough to share?"*

You might say, *"But how do I do it?"*

Simply be honest about your life.

Be open about the difference that Jesus has made.

Live a life worthy of your calling and people will see a difference. When they ask, *"What happened?"* answer:

> *"Because Jesus loved me enough to die for me, I love Him enough to obey Him. As I started obeying His Word, I began to change. The joy, the peace, the confidence, the difference that you see....it's because of Him."*

Here's one last component that I believe is important as we talk about our calling to be salt and light to the world around us. As we share our testimony, we need to be careful to practice what we are preaching. The world has seen more than enough examples of people who talk about being a Christian, but live like they don't care what Jesus thinks. Rather than making Jesus look like a shiny red apple, they make Christianity look like spoiled, rotten fruit that nobody wants to be around.

Part of accepting our purpose to fulfill the Great Commission is accepting the responsibility to represent Jesus well to the world. This can be so ridiculously practical.

For example, over a year ago I went to get a hair cut. I'd

gone to my usual spot, but something was off---the beautician seemed rushed and distracted. I tried to ignore it until she said I was finished and my reflection in the mirror looked nothing like the picture I'd given her.

Almost immediately I felt a mixture of panic and anger rising in my chest. It was taking every bit of the Holy Spirit's power inside of me to keep from spewing out words like: *"What have you done to my hair? How could you do such a bad job? Why couldn't you slow down and pay attention? You expect me to pay for this?"*

Thankfully, these and other unkinder things did not come out of my mouth. Why not? Because just about the time I was contemplating crying over my hair right there in the salon chair, the Holy Spirit reminded me that the salon was filled with people who knew I was a Christian. They knew that Jamie and I travel, telling people about Jesus and claiming to live a life representative of Him.

In almost a split second I was faced with a crossroads: overreact about the temporary problem of a bad haircut and risk damaging my witness or get over it, be kind, and wait until I was in the privacy of my car to deal with my emotions. That's when Christianity becomes really practical.....when you are in line at the grocery store, when you are stuck in traffic, when you're hungry, or tired, or when you have pms, or you just got a really bad haircut. Will you live out what you advertise when you say *"I'm a Christian?"*

I can't say it's easy, but I do think it's important. From time to time we need to ask ourselves:

"What if someone's eternal destiny is affected by my behavior, reactions, and attitudes?"

The world is watching....that's why it's important that we

recognize our lives are a living example of our testimony. It's important to leave them with a positive reflection of Christ.

What do we do when we fail?

Because even though we should strive to avoid sin at all costs, from time to time, we will fail. Whether we are rude to someone when we should be kind, let an expletive slip after we've slipped on the ice and fallen in the snow (true story), or even if we've made a dramatically bad choice that has damaged not only our reputation but other people's lives, there is still hope.

The world is watching....that's why it's important that we recognize our lives are a living example of our testimony.

You may be asking *"How? I blew my witness—where do I go from here?"*

I believe you start with open and honest repentance. Don't make excuses or try to justify what you did —just admit that you were wrong— that you sinned and you are sorry. Let the same people who saw you sin, see you repent. Don't just ask God to forgive you, but ask the people who you hurt for forgiveness as well. It's amazing how far humility and true repentance will go toward changing judgement to mercy and grace.

Of course, words will only go so far. After you repent, you need to demonstrate through your actions that you are changing. While I don't believe in penance for the sake of penance, I strongly believe in the value of restitution in an effort to restore what you've damaged. For instance, if you stole something, give it back. If you broke a relationship, do all that you can to heal it or at least see that the person you damaged is healed. Don't act like you believe that grace is cheap or forgiveness is automatic. Take responsibility for your actions, truly repent, and get back on the road to following Jesus.

How does this get you back on the road to fulfilling the Great Commission?

Well, even though it would have been better if you'd not have fallen, your choice to get back up and keep following Jesus demonstrates His grace, His mercy, His forgiveness and His ability to restore a broken life. If there's one thing that our world is looking for today, it is hope. Among all of the brokenness, the chaos, the wounded hearts, and the pain, they want to know that they can begin again.

This is the message of the Great Commission: Jesus came to save sinners. As we allow Him to work on our hearts and radically change our lives, we demonstrate this truth.

More than anything else, this is the purpose for which we were created: To make Jesus known to the world. To be salt and light everywhere we go and in everything that we do.

We are all called to fulfill the Great Commission. It isn't an option; it is a command. Perhaps the reason that so many are struggling to find their purpose in life is that they don't realize this is their purpose.

So here's my challenge to you: ***Ask the Holy Spirit how He wants you to start fulfilling this purpose. Then start doing it.***

Don't wait for the *"big door"* to open, but begin seeing the incredible mission field that is open to you every day…in your community….at your job….with your friends… and throughout your day.

Find your purpose in fulfilling the Great Commission. ***"By***

opening up to others, you'll prompt people to open up with God, this generous Father in heaven." (The Message, Matthew 5:16).

Study Questions:

1. What does this phrase mean to you: *"Present Jesus to the world like a shiny red apple—so appealing that they just can't wait to take a bite"*?
2. What are some practical ways that you can *"sprinkle the love of Jesus"* in your everyday life?
3. What does the story of the Samaritan woman teach us about being salt & light?
4. What is keeping you from sharing your testimony?
5. How do you feel about the line, *"Your testimony doesn't belong to you—it belongs to God. It is the story of His grace, His mercy, His compassion, and His miraculous power"*?
6. Why is it important that our lifestyle matches the words we speak about Jesus and Christianity?
7. What should we do to represent Jesus well when we make a mistake or sin?
8. What practical steps can you begin to take to fulfill the Great Commission in your world?

CONCLUSION

So here we are at the end of our journey. Even as we're preparing to wrap this up, I'm sure some of you are thinking, *"So these truths were great and all, but I still don't know what I'm supposed to DO."*

I understand. I've been right where you are…

…when I came home from college.

…during the many years when life didn't make any sense even though I knew I was in God's will.

...in the months after my mom passed away when my role of helping her ended.

....whenever one door was closing, and I needed to transition to another.

In these moments we're all tempted to focus on what we're going to ***do*** next rather than focusing on who we will ***be***.

Even though I don't know where you're coming from, I can't really answer the question of what's next for you. All I can do is bring you back to the truths that have held steady in my life whenever I'm searching for my own passion, place, and purpose.

Here they are:

Your first priority in life is to love Jesus and invest in your relationship with Him.

Absorb God's Word.

Embrace the people in your life and love them with all of your heart.

Whatever job or responsibility you have today, work at it with all of your heart as if you were working for Jesus.

Commit to living a life worthy of your calling. Abandon sin and pursue holiness.

Seek to advance God's kingdom first and foremost in every area of your life and in all that you do.

As you are faithful in these things, God will be faithful to lead you to His purposes for your life.

Along the way, be open to a change of plans. Don't get your heart set on the idea that *"it has to be this way."* Trust me, I can almost guarantee that God has some surprises in mind. That's what makes it an adventure!

Also, don't be surprised if God's purpose for your life today is different from what it was yesterday. It may even change again years from now. That's one of the beautiful things about life with Jesus—His plan is never stagnant. He'll always be helping you grow, change, and head off in new directions.

Don't let the change freak you out—-it's normal. God has different plans for your life during different seasons of your life. Still, your purpose and passion will always be the same: loving Jesus with all of your heart and following Him wherever He leads.

This is a truth that I'm learning to love in my own life. You see, contrary to the answer I would have given years ago when I thought I knew exactly what my life would hold, if you asked me now where I think I'll be five or ten years from now, I wouldn't have a specific answer. I've learned through a lifetime of ups and downs, twists and unexpected turns, and God-ordained surprises that the future is something none of us can guarantee.

I've also learned to be okay with that.

I think the key to this realization is that, in the deepest parts of my heart, I've settled the fact that ***I'm not what I do.*** As long as I am in the center of God's will for my life, I can choose to enjoy whatever job He gives me because what I do does not define me. Instead, my identity comes from being a child of God. My purpose is to love and obey Him and do whatever He wants during any time in my life.

It's like it says in Matthew 6:33, **"Seek the Kingdom of God above all else, and live righteously, and He will give you everything you need." (NLT).**

Proverbs 3:5-6 says, "Trust in the Lord with all your heart and lean not on your own understanding in all your ways submit to him, and He will make your paths straight." (NIV).

For me, these verses aren't just cliches that you pop out to give a Christian-ese answer. Rather, obeying them has helped me to find my passion, place, and purpose in life. I've learned that when I truly seek God and His will, He takes care of the how, the when, and the where.

Although today I don't know exactly what circumstances led you to pick up a book on finding your place in this world, nor do I know exactly what God's plan for your life may be, the one thing that I know beyond a shadow of a doubt is that He has a plan. As you commit to following the principles laid out in this book, He will be faithful to lead you and guide you to the place He wants you to be.

We started off our journey together with these words: **"For I know the plans I have for you,' declares the Lord, 'plans to prosper you and not to harm you, plans to give you hope and a future." (Jeremiah 29:11)**

As we close, this promise still holds true.

God has a purpose and plan for your life. He has a place specifically designed just for you. As you willingly submit your plans to His plans, He will lead you and guide you where He wants you to go.

Now the choice rests with you.

Are you willing to submit your will to God's will so that He can lead you to His plan and purpose for your life?

Are you willing to lay aside your preconceived ideas of what your life should look like and fully surrender to God's plans and purposes?

Are you willing to let the Holy Spirit show you who He wants you to be—-the real you that God originally created and designed for His purpose?

As He leads you to what He wants you to *"do,"* are you willing to fill your role in your family, your community, your church, and your world?

Most importantly, are you willing to learn to live a life worthy of your calling? Will you let the Holy Spirit make you into a new creation, preparing you for the work He wants to bring to full growth in your life?

These are the questions we need to answer day by day as we seek to find our passion, our place, and our purpose.

Along the way, try to enjoy the journey. Because here's the truth: the journey is your real life. Don't waste your days trying to get somewhere else, but instead, enjoy the full journey of where you are currently and where God is taking you.

Above all else, remember:

Your purpose is to have a relationship with your Heavenly Father and seek His will for your life.

Your passion should be Jesus, learning God's Word and applying it to your life.

Your place is wherever God leads you today. Don't waste your life worrying about tomorrow but live every moment to the fullest, right where God presently has you. Someday God may move you to a new venture or you may find that you've been living in your mission field all along, and God is just waiting for you to see it.

Remember: **"God can do anything, you know—far more than you could ever imagine or guess or request in your wildest dreams! He does it not by pushing us around but by working within us, his Spirit deeply and gently within us." (The Message, Ephesians 3:20).**

I can't wait to hear what He has planned for you!

Bibliography

Chapter 6

1. Castaway. Dir. Robert Zemeckis. Perf. Tom Hanks, Helen Hunt and Nick Searcy. 20th Century Fox and DreamWorks Pictures, 2000. Film.

Chapter 7

1. Richard Herritt is the author of the deliverance prayer. He is the leader of Herritt Spiritual Warfare Ministries, Inc., www.conquerors-in-christ.org

2. MacKenzie, Catherine. Can Brown Eyes be Made Blue? Christian Focus Publications, 2005.

Chapter 9

1. Friday, Francesca, "More Americans Are Single Than Ever Before— And They're Healthier, Too" Observer. January 16, 2018. https://observer.com/2018/01/more-americans-are-single-than-ever- before-and-theyre-healthier-too/.

Chapter 11

1. Princess Diaries. Dir. Garry Marshall. Perf. Julie Andrews, Anne Hathaway, Hector Elizondo, Heather Matarazzo, Mandy Moore, Caroline Goodall, and Robert Schwartzman. Walt Disney Home Entertainment, 2001. Film.

We all crave significance. Adessa Holden's book

FINDING SIGNIFICANCE

will help you understand how God sees you, that he loves to speak hope and new life into those that the world sees as insignificant. Each chapter provides questions for reflection, making it a wonderful tool for self or small group study.

Visit **www.adessaholden.com** for details.

Also available in both print and digital formats from Amazon, BarnesandNoble.com, and other online retailers.

We're all just a little bit broken.

We all have areas from our past, from choices we've made, or from circumstances that we've lived through that have caused us pain and heartache in our lives.

The good news is that we don't have to stay trapped in our brokenness. Through the power of the Holy Spirit and practicing the Biblical principles of healing, each of us can experience victory, freedom, and the abundant life that Jesus has for us.

Visit **www.adessaholden.com** for details.

Also available in both print and digital formats
from Amazon, BarnesandNoble.com,
and other online retailers.

ABOUT THE AUTHOR

Adessa Holden is an ordained minister with the Assemblies of God specializing in women's ministry. She's the author of the Finding Healing Curriculum including *"Finding Healing"*, *"The Finding Healing Workbook"*, and the *"Finding Healing Video Series."* She's also written *"Finding Significance"* and several e-books.

Whether it be speaking, writing, blogging, or teaching through videos, Adessa's passion is helping women develop an intimate, personal relationship with Jesus and become the women God originally designed them to be.

Adessa is also the Vice-President/Treasurer of 4One Ministries. Together with her brother, Jamie, they travel the East Coast speaking, holding conferences and producing Men's and Women's Resources that provide practical Biblical teaching to strengthen, encourage, and challenge individuals to grow in their walk with Christ and apply Biblical principles to their everyday life.

When asked about herself she'll tell you, *"I'm a women's minister, a sister and a daughter. I love to laugh and spend time with people. My favorite things are chocolate, anything purple, summertime (because I can wear sandals), and riding in the car listening to music (which is a good thing since I spend so much time traveling). It is my absolute honor and privilege to serve Jesus and women through this ministry."*

Adessa Holden can be contacted at adessa@adessaholden.com, where she welcomes any questions, comments, or requests for speaking engagements.

To read more from Adessa, visit: www.adessaholden.com

Made in the USA
Middletown, DE
30 March 2019